MW00988539

Published in the United States of America.

ISBN-13: 978-1539479512
ISBN-10: 153947951X

First paperback edition.

The Power of Practice
Spiritual Laws for an Extraordinary You
by Julianna Ricci

Quantum Imprint
Rhode Island

THE POWER OF PRACTICE

Spiritual Laws for an Extraordinary You

by Julianna Ricci

TABLE OF CONTENTS

INTRODUCTION

The Path to Receiving

> *The law of attraction works universally on every plane of action, and we attract whatever we desire or expect.*
>
> -1897, Ralph Trine, *In Tune With the Infinite*

Yes to this!

Yes, a hundred, thousand, million times over.

Yes!!!

And...*it's just not that simple*.

Say what?

I know, I know. The law of attraction is delicious. It feels good—in fact it feels unbelievably great!

And let me say right up front that I am an ardent believer in the deep, cosmic workings of it.

It's just that... *it's not quite enough.*

You likely have heard that before, or even experienced for yourself that there's more to the law of attraction than meets the eye.

This book was written—pretty much through me—as the final deciphering of that law of attraction puzzle that has so many of us stumped.

Here's the thing. There are millions, likely billions, of us—and I include myself because I am still a student of this lifelong process—wanting to create something different in our lives. We want a better job, partner, house, body, bank account, attitude, car, outlook. We know we are meant for more, and boy have we been trying! We have been busting our butts—believing, intending, visualizing, studying, dieting, exercising, dating, you name it.

And yet, despite our valiant efforts, we still haven't gotten to where we want to be.

Which leads me the overarching premise of this book: How diligently have you been practicing?

I know the knee-jerk answer, because it's the same

one I used to give: "*All. The. Time.*"

But now let me get more specific. How much dedicated, uninterrupted, come hell-or-high-water time, energy, and focus have you put toward this thing you desire? Each day? Each week? Each month? Each year?

As much as a high school wrestler? An Olympic swimmer? A Wall Street executive? A Master?

My guess is that your answer has now become, "Eh, when you put it that way... maybe not so much."

That was my answer, too.

And while I don't intend to become that intense anytime soon, my belief in the ultimate Power of Practice has only grown in the time that it has been tapping on my shoulder.

You see, this book began as a whisper, then became a nudge. Eventually I listened, and I wrote. And the more I spent time with the idea, the more I came to see that Practice is the critical foundation for manifesting our desires.

These pages have become a very practical approach to finally, once and for all, mastering your powers of manifestation. If you follow this book, you will need no others. You will get the life of your dreams. I know that's a big statement. I also know it to be true.

Because here's the thing: this book is different.

It's an amalgamation of logic and instinct, practicality and intuitiveness, discipline and love. It is a balancing of two ways of being, and it is this very balancing that gives it such extraordinary power.

It is also a real, working guide. It literally takes you, step by step, through your journey. The Power of Practice contains a lot of the work I do individually with my private clients. I can't coach everyone, so this book is my best attempt at sharing the insights and the "secrets" with as many people as possible. It will guide you through the process of aligning with your highest energies, so that as you choose and commit to your practice from the most power-filled place inside of you.

Because the more of us who step into our power in this way, the better we all will be. It sounds corny, I know. But it is true on the deepest of levels.

As we raise our individual vibration, so too we raise the collective vibration.

Please know that nothing in this book is difficult. It only asks two things of you:

1. That you believe you already have what it takes to live the life of your dreams.

2. That you choose to take action.

As I said, neither is difficult. However, they do require some effort. Because if we're to be honest, the path to "the life of our dreams" is rarely, if ever, an effortless journey. In my down moments, I have wondered why the Universe would be that cruel. In my aligned moments, I know the Universe is not cruel at all, but rather entirely and limitlessly benevolent.

You see, the effort—the work, the picking-ourselves-up-and-dusting-ourselves-off commitment, the belief, the practice—are all part of the journey itself. They're part of the beauty. They are a gift in and of themselves.

Because it is along the path of this journey that we discover our strength, our super-powers.

This is arguably the entire reason for us becoming human in the first place.

This book exists to guide you on these next steps of your journey. It's here to help you open even further to the fullness of your own gifts and to the abundance in which you're meant to live.

As you follow the insights of this book, you will become the exceedingly powerful, love-filled, successful, deliberate alchemist of your magnificent life.

In gratitude,
Julianna

CHAPTER ONE

The Significance of Balance

> *Nothing is static. There is potential
> in everything. When you decide to
> make change, all the forces in the
> Universe begin to conspire in
> your favor.*

I met James in 2000, shortly after he'd completed his PhD at the University of Cambridge. A brilliant man, to be certain. Maybe even too smart for his own good. To say he was stuck in his head, with little access to his heart, would be an understatement. I didn't fault him for it, because I knew it wasn't for lack of trying. It was simply because his life was so hard, at such an early age, that the walls he had built were of great height and even greater fortitude. In fact, the strength of his walls were a testament to his extraordinary power.

We began the work of coaching in 2008, and I watched him slowly connect to aspects of himself he hadn't accessed since he was a child. The more creative, feeling aspects. And as time went on, a balance between his left and right brains emerged.

Then, in 2012, James was diagnosed with a rare blood cancer. He was given a 15% chance of survival.

Yep. That's fifteen percent. Not odds any of us would like.

As he worked with the doctors tending to his physical body, he doubled down on his inner work—and a change occurred that can only be described as miraculous.

Not only did James survive physically, he grew spiritually and emotionally in ways that were magical to witness. Skeptics might say it was simply the realization of his own mortality that changed James, and surely, that was part of it. But I saw James do the work. I saw him actively integrating what we had done together, opening in ways he had never opened before, and becoming the best, most grounded and loving human he could be.

And it worked. Today, James listens to his heart before he listens to his head. He makes choices that are expansive not just for him, but for the people around him. He uses his brilliance and strength to bring goodness not just into the world, but into everyone he touches. He is more successful now than he's ever been.

The way his life transformed affirmed for me that I'd done the right thing when I'd answered the calling to coach.

James himself puts it this way:

For the first time in my life, my heart truly opened to the realm of my full potential and the possibilities for the present, which is always the future. I began painting again, writing creatively, and meditating, not to mention exploring alternative personal and professional paths that would have seemed ridiculous when I finished my PhD. I began to recognize the significance of balance, true balance, where both head and heart are fully motivated by spirit and truth.

My future no longer reveals itself as I had envisioned, the journey is now wide open as I have fully embraced letting go, allowing, and accepting the now, in every moment of every day. I may have only met with Julianna on occasion, but the conversations, the work, the readings, and the exercises were the seeds that have become the full-fledged forest of life that is now me.

The path you'll embark on with Julianna is unimaginable from the outset, and if you're like me when I began the work, your logical/rational brain may not be able to wrap your head around what she does, or how.

Stop.

Let Go.

If you let go to take the path, the other side is inconceivable, but more real than anything you'll ever do in your life.

What is Practice?

We all know the basic definition of the word practice: you repeat an action, again and again, in order to get better at it.

That's part of it, to be sure.

But this book also adds the equally important aspect of your "Practice" (with a capital P) as *the activity itself.*

Depending on your goal or dream, you might choose (with the help of the exercises in this book) your Practice to be exercising, being more thoughtful with your spouse, taking steps toward your dream career, or manifesting your way wealth, health, or any number of desires.

So really, what we're talking about here is the art of consistently *practicing your Practice.*

Stick around—I think you're going to find this not just fun and easy, but also gorgeously transformational.

Enjoy!

CHAPTER TWO

The Way = Practice

*As you ask for guidance, it will
make itself found.*

There are literally hundreds of books out there about
how to make new habits or get motivated. Why on
earth would I choose to write another one? Especially
when I am not a certified expert on behavior change
theory or strategies?

I was once an expert in marine biology. I am currently
an expert in Energy Alchemy and Coaching. I strive
daily to be an expert at mothering two amazing boys.
I am definitely an expert at listening. But I can't
justifiably claim to be an expert on the ins and outs of
behavior change.

But I wrote this book anyway. Why?

First, think about James's story. I get chills when I do. The change in his life was so complete, it was a rebirth in every sense of the term. And while James had access to my coaching, I understand that not everyone does. I want to help change as many lives as possible. A book is a simple, easily-affordable way to expand these changes out into the world.

Second, this book mostly wrote itself. It was the unplanned—but not unwanted—child that insisted upon coming through into the physical world.

Third, and the main reason I "agreed" to write it, is that nearly every one of the existing books on behavior change are too left-brained—too blocky and analytical—for a huge population. That population, I realized, consists of my people.

Who are my people?

My people are those of us on a spiritual path, in some form or another, who know we want more for our lives. We've tried many approaches, but haven't quite been able to create the results of our dreams.

The behavior-change books are not written in a way my people understand. I mean sure, we understand the words. Of course we do. But the approach, the tone, the vibration—they just don't land in our awareness in any meaningful way. They don't get the job done, because they don't speak to the deep places of our truest knowing.

At the same time, the super New-Age-y and 'woo-woo' books aren't working either. They sound good, and they feel good, and they resonate deeply on an important level. But they haven't actually produced the results we so determinedly seek.

There must be, I realized, a middle ground. There must be a way to combine the best of the "pound the pavement until stuff works" and the "think and it will be so" schools of thought.

So I wrote this book from that exact middle ground, from the place I know represents the missing link for my people.

There's another key reason. At the same time that there are hundreds of habit-changing books, there are now thousands of self-help, law of attraction, manifestation books out there. And I am so glad there are! They've opened up awareness, on a global level, of some of the most profound concepts of our existence.

I remember when *The Secret* first came out—talk about making amazing, life-changing concepts accessible to the masses! It was a god-send, to have so many people start speaking in this language of possibility and manifestation. I was elated!

The trouble, I soon found, is that the book merely scratched the surface of what is really happening with our powers of manifestation.

And in doing so, it set a lot of hopeful, excited people forth on a path that never quite materialized. Many are still seeking, attempting the same concepts put forth in that original book, or in the multitude of similar books that have followed.

The real motivating force for me saying "yes" to this book was to offer these people—my people—a way out of this frustrating cycle of believing, trying, and not reaching the goal.

I know all too well how it feels to be in there. Painful, disheartening, draining. There were many times I lost my faith—in my powers of manifestation, and in the Universe.

And then something happened.

Journal Entry, August 2014:

"A book has been nudging at me for the better part of the last six months. I've done my best to ignore it."

You see, the last two manuscripts I wrote still sit upon my bookshelf. I didn't even finish the first, which is fine because it let me release negative energy. My second gone-nowhere manuscript is also collecting dust on my bookshelf. It, at least, is complete. It too was therapeutic, and I believe its day will come.

Given this history of manuscript-abandonment, I couldn't help but feel a whole lot of ducking and dodging when yet another book came knocking on my consciousness. I was doing a great job of pushing it away until, for no reason whatsoever, I happened to pull that second manuscript off the shelf.

And there, in flashing neon colors (not literally, of course—but it might as well have been), was one final message for me about this new darned book. In bold letters on the first page of Manuscript #2 were the words:

The Way = Practice.

The way is practice? Really? *Really?* You've got to be kidding me.

Because here's the thing: this book—the one that you're holding right now—has been called *The Power of Practice* ever since it first came rapping on my mental door. It's always wanted to be called that - and at that moment it became exceedingly clear to me that, after half a year of hiding from it, this book was in charge—not me.

I know what I originally meant, two years ago, when I wrote, "The Way = Practice."

I meant that the key for me, and for the realization of all of my dreams and goals, was to keep up a spiritual practice. That was the message I received loud and clear through the entirety of writing Manuscript #2. All the things I was looking for and trying to manifest—those would come to me through a dedicated, disciplined spiritual practice. By

connecting with my higher self on a regular basis, I'd
be tapping into great power. The Great Power. From
there, all things are possible. From there, all
manifestation occurs. I still know this to be true.

The Way = Practice.

It also meant, back then, that the journey, not just the
results, were my reward. By keeping up a spiritual
practice I'd enter into bliss regularly, as I do each
time I connect with my higher self. By becoming a
channel in that way, I feel good and tingly and
expansive inside.

So the Way to all those lovely, wonderful feelings?
Meditate. Go into sacred space, regularly. Practice.

The Way = Practice.

But when I saw these words again on that fateful
August morning in 2014, their final meaning came
through as a direct message from a higher place: my
way forward was to write this book, "The Power of
Practice." And so, I gave up the ducking and dodging,
and finally allowed these pages to come through.

That said, I believe you manifested these pages just as
surely as I did. They are something that you called
into being, without even consciously knowing it, in
order to support you on your journey. You've come to
the place where you are now, on your path, and you
are ready for this next step. All your previous efforts
have brought you here. Each and every one of them

has steered you to this point on the map where
are now. They have prepared you for this next, big
step of your journey.

You're here for a reason.

Every single one of you reading this book has
something very specific and important to offer the
world.

I know this as surely as I know my name. You are
here, in this book, because you have a unique gift to
bring to the world.

You.

You reading these words in this exact moment. I
might not know what your particular gift is, but I
know it is your gift. And I know for certain that your
gift is filled with power, and that it's moving through
you, trying to come into the world, in a way that
almost defies explanation. Your gift might be big, or it
might be small. It doesn't matter - not in the least. It
only matters that it is your gift. You are being guided
and supported in creating it. That is why you are right
here, right now, in this very moment.

I also know that your gift is meant to see the light of
day. It is meant to come through. And as you find a
way to allow your gift to manifest, you are benefitting
the world. You are, as I like to say, "uplifting the
collective vibration." Every single time one of us
achieves a dream, we are aligning with universal

power, and allowing it to flow through us into this physical world. Imagine that: bringing divine energy through you and into the world. There is nothing—truly, *no thing*—better that we can do.

Nothing.

I want—more than anything—to see you succeed. I want it for you. I want it for those around you. I want it so that you can share this process - your success! - with all whom you touch, so that possibility and dreams can come alive in their hearts as well. I want it for the collective Us, for as each of us shifts our own thoughts, lives, and vibrations into 'I can,' we invariably turn to those around us, and intentionally or otherwise, lift them up as well.

Wow. And yes!

So here's the deal: the book in your hands is magical.

It might not appear that way at first glance, because it's a book about action. But that action is balanced with deep spiritual truths.

First, the action. Aside from the obvious—of introducing you to some new perspectives and realities about manifestation—I also set out to walk you through the process of not just choosing a Practice, but also setting yourself up so that you can't help but succeed.

In order to do this, we cover all the bases. I'll be

showing you a number of key new ways of understanding your relationship to manifesting all that you desire—as well as helping you uncover and remove the hidden blocks that are holding you back. I know a lot of people talk about these things, but this book is different in two ways: 1) we shift your energy in order to shift you into a new way of being, and 2) I'm actually asking you to do some work as you go through the book.

In our case, the work is fun and easy. It involves a handful of exploratory writing exercises, so that you actively shift any old patterns that are keeping your dreams just out of reach.

Imagine that by reading a mere eighteen chapters and doing a handful of easy, rewarding exercises, you can become a master manifestor. That's what the book, the explanations, the encouragement—and at times the nudging—are here for.

Second, in terms of how this book is magical, I have put my decade of Energy Coaching—and the ingredients of my special coaching sauce—into these pages. My coaching is unique, and given the feedback I have received from countless clients, I dare say it is magical. It is the gift I have been given in this life. As you proceed through these pages, I will be sharing that gift for your benefit.

Third, I have very deliberately infused the book with a heightened energy and vibration, to help shift you from where you are now into where you dream of being. I have had some very powerful friends imbue it with their powers as well.

And finally, I believe 100% that I was asked to write this book specifically because each and every one of you sent a signal to the Universe, asking for the real secret behind manifestation. I was merely a conduit for brining you that not-so-secret secret.

So yes, this book is special. And magical.

It will change your world, forever.

I am delighted it has found you.

CHAPTER THREE

The Way

Mistakes are like love;
never be afraid to invest in either.

I want to give it all away. Right now. I want to give
you that very secret, the missing link, the key that has
been keeping real manifestation just out of reach for
you and so many others. It was kept out of my reach
for a long time as well.

Most books make you wait. That doesn't work for
me, though. I understand why they do it; they want to
make sure you're engaged enough—hooked into the
process or product—so that you won't just grab the
secret and then walk away.

Do me a favor and promise yourself that you will
keep reading, even after I give you the secret. Why?

Because the secret is only as good as the information that follows it. If you just take the secret and close the book, it will do you no good whatsoever. You might as well not even know it in the first place.

On the contrary, if you learn the secret and then keep reading, I can guarantee you that your life will change.

Agreed?

Okay, good.

Here's the secret:

The Way = Practice.

No joke.

Yeah, I kind of let the 'ole cat out of the bag by telling you that exact same thing in the last chapter, didn't I? Or we could say that the truth was hiding in plain sight, or some other cliche. But remember, you promised to stay with me!

I understand that the idea of practice is not sexy. And I suspect it might have caused you to deflate a little, when what you really wanted was to expand. I get it. That's how I felt when I first realized this.

Sigh.

But that doesn't change the facts.

And the fact is, the secret is to practice.

See, I tried the sexier approaches for a long time. You know the ones I'm talking about—the ones where you just have to think, or believe, in order to receive. I tried those for nearly a decade. And then I realized it just plain wasn't working.

It finally dawned on me that it wasn't the Law of Attraction that was failing me—it was my commitment to it, or lack thereof, that was failing me.

I had been leaving out the most critical part: practice.

Without practice, none of my manifestation efforts could ever succeed. My "thoughts become reality" belief system sure felt good—heck, it felt great! Sexy, beautiful, true—even a bit mysterious and cosmic. I loved everything about it.

Except that I couldn't actually get it to work.

My sincerest hope for you, dear reader, is that you choose to balance the sexy (Law of Attraction) with the solid (Practice).

This book is my most heart-felt attempt to walk you through that process of becoming committed—once and for all—to sticking with your Practice.

I am here to support you along the way. It is not easy to do this work—and it's even harder to do it alone. If you will just stick with the book, and commit to what

it has to offer, I fully believe you will finally—
finally—be able to manifest the life of your dreams.

And want to know the great news? Although the
concept of "practice" may not seem so sexy, the
results of your practice—of getting, doing and being
what you know you're meant to get, do and be—are
as sexy as sexy can be!

Basic Truths

There are three big truths upon which this book is
built. These truths are touched upon in many other
books, but nowhere (to my knowledge) have they
been presented as the pivotal and intricately-linked
foundations I have come to know them to be.

Basic Truth #1:

The true power of practice begins in the non-physical
realms. Everything that we're speaking about, when
we talk of manifestation, has its roots in the unseen.

*All things that we experience here in the physical
world do indeed begin as thought.*

(If you thought my "secret" from earlier was not sexy
enough, then here's where I make up for it. Not only
did I give away the "secret" in the very first chapter,
but I'm now launching into some hard-core how-the-
Universe-works stuff right out of the gates. We go

deeper into it later, but we need this stuff to get us started.)

See, here's how the whole "thoughts become reality" thing goes down:

Just as a house gets built one stone at a time, so too our manifestations get built one thought—or intention, belief, affirmation—at a time. As long as they are receiving focused attention, they are being built in the energetic form, stone by stone.

I want to illustrate this concept by introducing you to my friend, Ken Elliot. Ken is an extremely talented landscape painter, and also a master manifestor. He wrote his book, *Manifesting 123*, based largely on what he learned from working with a fellow friend, Judy Goodman, who is a highly-skilled psychic.

Ken was in the early stages of wrapping his head around the fact that Judy received messages, images, and information from 'the other side.' One of Judy's particular skills is that she is telepathic, meaning that she can read, hear, or see others' thoughts—especially those that are sent directly to her. Ken was somewhat skeptical at this seemingly impossible feat. So he decided to test it out.

He experimented numerous times with 'sending' Judy a thought, and each time she 'received' it. What made it even more intriguing to Ken was that she would actually 'see' whatever he sent, as if it were literally forming in front of her.

So on her birthday, when Ken sent her a yellow rose—simply by thinking of a yellow rose and directing the thought to Judy—she literally saw a yellow rose forming in front of her eyes.

And when he 'sent' her a "5-foot tall Daffy Duck... holding a vertical stick about 3 feet tall" with a board attached, and the word love written in red lipstick?

Here is what Judy saw: "Well, what I'm looking at is some 2 ½ foot tall, poor human-ey thing. It's got skinny little arms and legs with cartoon colors on it, so I figured it's a cartoon character and it's got a stick in its hand."

Judy saw Ken's thought forming in a sort of ethereal fog in front of her.

So yeah, there's that. (And a lot more about this later in Chapter 12.)

What does this story have to do with you and your dreams? It means that all the affirmation, Law of Attraction, goal-setting, list-making, visualizing stuff is for real.

Why? Because our thoughts are real and they create things. They can be transferred through time and space, and they create form. These forms are visible to those, like Judy, who are skilled enough to see into the non-physical realms.

In other words, our thoughts are creating form in the

non-physical realm. This is where all manifestation begins.

Basic Truth #2:

Manifestations materialize when we hold our focus— our thoughts, intentions, beliefs, affirmations—long enough for them to come through into the physical world.

The house we talked about a few moments ago? It will manifest in physical form when we continue to build it one stone at a time. Only when its blueprint is fully formed in the non-physical can it appear here, in the 3D physical world. Anything you've ever created in your life—whether through your own 'effort' or through seemingly random events—appeared because enough thought (and belief) was placed upon it, for a long enough period of time.

On the flip side, this Basic Truth also means that if we prematurely abandon our goals, dreams, or intentions, then they lose their power. They face the same fate that an unfinished house faces in the physical world. Over time it would start falling apart and eventually just completely disintegrate.

So too our manifestations. When we abandon them before they are complete, they remain intact for a spell, but without further focused intention—without further energy and direction from their maker (you and your deliberate thoughts/creation), they begin to crumble. They never become what you set out for them to be.

What this means to us—all the believers and enthusiastic followers of the law of attraction, myself included—is that the single-most important thing we can do is hold our focused attention on our dream and keep it there.

And by that I mean to have a Practice around the dream—whether it's action-oriented steps, or visualizations, or some other effort—that we stay with day in and day out, month in and month out. We stay with it even when we don't see it manifesting, because we know that it is taking shape in the non-physical, and will come through into the physical when it's complete.

There is great power in this realization. It is beautiful and inspiring. It confirms that when we focus and believe, when we stay with something and visualize it daily, when we intend and affirm, we really are able to manifest whatever our minds can imagine. It is also extraordinarily empowering. It means that you, and you alone, have the power to create your reality. It is up to you, and no one else, to do this work.

Basic Truth # 3:

Because we are not yet masters, we must also take action.

If we were absolute masters at creating from thought, then Basic Truths #1 & 2 would be enough. However, for a number of reasons that are largely outside of our control, we are not yet masters (more on this later).

For now, the reality is that we must also take action in the physical world. And our action must be a parallel effort—both in topic and in consistency—to our visualizations, thoughts, dreams. They must match up, or else we work against ourselves.

These Basic Truths may indeed seem basic. And taken alone, they are.

The magic happens when we learn to abide by them not one at a time, but in unison, as a collective whole.

When we miss this subtle, but crucial fact, we seem to continually fall short of our dreams.

On the flip side, when we learn to combine them, in equal measure, there truly is no limit to what we can do, be or have.

CHAPTER FOUR

Dreams and Pendulums

We do not experience the world as beautiful because it is; rather, it becomes beautiful because that is what we expect of it.

At 32 years of age, Bea was not experiencing the world as beautiful. Not even close.

A breakup six months prior had left her so devastated that she felt always on the verge of tears. She was addicted to sugar and unhappy with her weight. As she attests, "I had never before felt so stuck in sadness."

When Bea came to me for coaching, her dream was simple: she just wanted to feel okay again.

In our very first coaching sessions, I was thrilled to see Bea release so much of the sadness and hurt she'd been carrying, and over the course of a year, her life moved dramatically in a wonderful direction. She changed careers (a huge feat, given the massive success she had achieved in her previous work), changed her way of eating and lost 15 pounds, and moved on from the sadness surrounding her breakup and into a place of embracing her power as a single, strong female.

In short, she far exceeded her simple dream of just feeling okay again.

If you haven't yet noticed, I am a big fan of dreams. I get inordinately thrilled when I hear about other people living out their dreams—even small ones. I can literally feel the vibrations of a benevolent Universe manifesting itself in their story as they tell it.

I feel the same tingling sensation when I go into my own dream-building space. In my mind I see and feel that my dreams have come true. Sometimes I'm a little embarrassed by the joy it brings me—likely because I can hear so many nay-sayers snickering about what a hopeless dreamer I am. But I know and deeply believe in the value of this type of heightened vibration; it is what brings us together with our dreams.

I also want to admit to the times that I have been a non-believer, either because I hadn't seen my dreams come true and I lost faith, or because I spent too much time and energy on the normal way of manifestation (e.g. working my butt off on task lists with little or no time spent on the visualizing, believing, and dreaming).

I have often found myself, over the past decade or so, feeling like a pendulum. When one "way of being" wasn't working, I would drop it, and swing to the other.

What I now understand on a very deep level is that in both cases—when I was on either side of that giant pendulum-swing—I was simply out of balance. I was doing too much of the one way, and not enough of the other. Trust me when I say it was a very frustrating decade! It still happens from time to time, but thankfully, with the gift of awareness, it now passes much more quickly.

Why am I sharing this?

First, because I wonder if the same has happened (or is currently happening) to you. And second, because once I finally cracked the code, or found the recipe, I felt like I had found the road map that I didn't even know I was looking for.

I've put that roadmap to work with clients like Bea, and I've put it into this book, in the form of exercises that afford you an opportunity to make real shifts in your life and in what you want to manifest. I encourage you to take the exercises as they come.

Follow the instructions to the best of your ability and be as thorough as you can. By digging into these exercises together, we're going to move your energy for you. And, as you'll see, energy-movement is a critical piece of this whole puzzle.

As we move forward, you'll notice the exercises are divided into two categories: Looking In and Digging Deeper. Neither is more important than the other. They work symbiotically, exploring ideas I've discussed in the Looking In sections, then Digging Deeper to really make the changes stick.

If the exercises aren't for you, I get it. We're all entering this book at different places, so some of you may find them ground-breaking, and others might not. I do highly recommend that you read each chapter nonetheless, since simply "being with" the energy of it will shift you in some pretty amazing ways. If you are desperate to decide upon your practice and get started, then skip ahead—and good luck!

For those of you who are feeling ready to make the most of the power this book has to offer, make sure you gather your tools: a journal and a pen.

If you take any *one* thing from this book, my hope is that it's the commitment to take consistent, long-term action. That action begins here, now.

A few quick tips for writing—which will begin in the next chapter—during the course of this book:

- Don't worry about spelling, grammar, punctuation, etc.

- Don't edit. Just write. Stream-of-consciousness style—as in, write whatever comes to mind and don't stop until you run out of things to write.

- Write as if no one will read it. Ever.

How do those sound to you? If they seem difficult to agree to, just do your best. Pretend you're a kid writing to Santa; you didn't worry about anything except for all the thoughts that were in your head. Do the same thing here. Get the thoughts out, no-holds-barred.

Let's get started!

CHAPTER FIVE

The Recipe

Balance allows flow. Flow allows magic. Magic allows success.

Who doesn't love a recipe? Ingredients all spelled out, trial-and-error tested by pros—all good stuff!

Take a look at these:

Recipe A

Goals + Discipline + Flexibility = Success

Recipe B

Dreams + Consistent, long-term action + Flow = Manifestation

These are clearly not recipes for cupcakes.

(Well, you know, unless your dream is to become a successful cupcake baker. Then they pretty much are. But I digress…)

They are recipes for success.

Recipes for living the life of your dreams.

They say the same thing, just in different "languages."

Which one feels better to you? It might be strange to realize, but the one that makes you twitch is the one that causes someone else to feel grounded, capable, and expanded. And conversely, the recipe that feels good and do-able to them, may feel totally off-center to you.

We are all different. We may be looking for the same things (love, joy, abundance, peace), but as I said before, we are all coming from very different places on our journeys. We have different ways of processing, understanding and creating. Naturally, what fits for one will not fit for another. And this is perfectly okay.

Take a look again at these recipes for success. Look at the individual pieces—these are the ingredients. These are the key pieces to becoming what you want—to having, being, or doing anything that you desire. Taken alone the ingredients are simple. The important part is to have, and use in the right quantities, each and every one of them.

Let's see where you are with your own ingredients.

Grab your pen and journal...

Looking In:

1. Write down each of those two recipes at the beginning of the chapter.

2. Put a star next to the one that looks, feels or sounds best to you.

3. Underline the word(s) (ingredients) that feel best to you, the one(s) that feel easy and exciting.

These are your naturals, the ones you are drawn to, the ones you can accomplish with your eyes closed. They bring you joy and excitement, and they have a lot to offer as we move forward with the changes we're making. They're likely the ones you've been turning to, as you work to create the life of your dreams.

For me, I tend to start with a heavy dose of "dreams" and "flow," (or goals and flexibility) but leave out "consistent, long-term action." How about you?

When we look at these concepts as if they're part of a

recipe, we see a valuable parable for how we need the right "ingredients," in the right quantities, mixed together in the right way, in order to make what we want.

You know how this goes: you're baking a cake and you put in too much flour, or too few eggs, or heaven-forbid too much salt or baking soda (can you tell I have personal experience with this one?!), and it all goes to pot. This is what I call a Broken Recipe.

And a Broken Recipe is almost worse than no recipe at all. I mean, imagine how it feels to bake some brownies, get all excited for their chocolatey gooey-ness, perhaps even plan to share them with friends and family—only to have them come out completely wrong. Turns out, you left out the butter, and now you and you're loved ones are sadly disappointed.

As you can surely see, this is how it goes with pursuing our dreams. If we don't have all the ingredients in place, we are putting in a mighty effort, but simply can't create the masterpiece that we desire. This has been holding so many of us back, without even realizing it. It is frustrating and exhausting to say the least, and can cause a serious loss of faith as more and more time passes.

If you've been trying and trying, but always coming up short, it's likely that you're not quite getting the recipe right.

Digging Deeper:

Revisit your response to Items 1 through 3 in LOOKING IN above. Think for a moment: which ingredient might you have left out while pursuing your goals or dreams? It's likely the one you flinched at, the one that zapped your energy or triggered some resistance. Take a good look, allow yourself to feel, and be completely honest with yourself. If none of them create this type of response, ask yourself which one generates the least excitement or positive feeling for you. Put a circle around whichever one filtered to the top (or the bottom, as the case may be).

This is the ingredient that has, to date, been holding you back. It's in there — I know it is.

How do I know?

Because there must be a missing ingredient in your recipe, or you would already be living the life of your dreams!

I'm going to guess that many of you, like me, circled "Discipline" or "Consistent, long-term action" as your missing ingredient.

Yes?

If so, you're in the right place. This book is for us— for you, me, and everyone else who has spent years adding heaps of beautiful, expansive "Dreams" and "Flow", but have unwittingly left out the key ingredient of Practice (read: 'discipline' or 'consistent, long-term action').

It's simply not enough to sprinkle a little Practice in every now and again—that's not what the real recipe calls for. It calls for Practice in equal measure to dreams and flow.

Equal parts.

Not just when we feel like it. Not just when we can get around to it. And not just when we can fit it in between our other suite of commitments.

I know, I know—not sexy, not fun. But it is un-leave-out-able.

See, it's not that we're not talented enough, or committed enough, or connected enough. It's not that we don't dream big enough, believe strongly enough, or attract hard enough. It's simply that we've been working with a Broken Recipe.

I, for one, decided that I was done with that nonsense.

I hope you are at the same place—that you're ready to begin working with the real secret sauce. This book is about putting that key ingredient back in—and doing it in a way that feels easy and downstream. The Way is Practice. As we add a dedicated Practice into our lives, we complete our recipe. And a Practice it is—day in and day out, week in and week out, month in and month out.

But wait…

Some of you may be feeling left behind. You may be going, 'Hold on, Julianna—that's not me!'

If it happens that you circled "flow" or "dreams," you're still in the right place! This book will absolutely help you to unlock those dreams, and to convince yourself of how important those "softer" things actually are. It will help you to move your energy, so that you come into a place of balance— your own particular form of balance.

Because that's what we're really talking about, right? Striking a real, lasting balance.

That is power.

CHAPTER SIX

My "Aha!" and the Scale

> *Be as a tree when the winds of*
> *change blow. Bend and bow with*
> *grace, for the winds will come and*
> *we choose to dance or break.*

A few years back, I had an 'Aha!' moment that went something like this:

I'm feeling down. Frustrated. Focusing on all the changes I've been intending/attracting/visualizing in my life that haven't come to fruition. It feels like the clock is ticking. Like I've already been gifted an overtime, and if I don't score soon, the buzzer buzzes and it's all over. And then it's time to throw in the towel, to stop chasing these pie-in-the-sky dreams, and go back to a "real" job.

Clearly, I'm not feeling at the top of my game. I'm aware of this fact, so I graciously gift myself a bit of space for a pity party. (That which we resist, persists. So as often as I remember, I intentionally anti-resist. You probably know it better as "allowing.") If I let this feeling-sorry-for-myself moment do its thing, I reason, I'll be better off than if I resist it.

I'll let it go for a day or two—that's all I'm giving it. I'm putting my foot down, Universe. I know these low vibrations aren't helping me achieve my dreams, but to heck with it—nothing else that I'm doing seems to work either.

I hate it when I get to this point, where it feels like there are no bootstraps left to pull up. I've done so much pulling over the years, I've nearly torn those suckers right off.

So I'm all ticked off.

I'm angry at god.

At the Universe.

At this path that's supposed to be for my highest good, and is meant to serve others.

There's nothing good about it though—it just keeps kicking me in the pants, again and again. I start scanning back through these years of trying and failing, trying and failing. So much work and conviction I've put into manifesting the life of my dreams.

I start thinking, 'I have put so much heart and soul into this, time and tears, and what do I have to show for it? Nothing. Nada.'

Next thought: 'Yeah, really, what has changed for me in these years of believing in the Law of Attraction, practicing visualization, keeping a positive vibration? Nothing, that's what! My house is still the same, only more worn down because of the passing years. There's been no major financial breakthrough. I've not "met" my Higher Self — despite many, many attempts, courses, books, and meditations. And while my relationships are fine, they're not the fabulous, expansive, over-the-top things I am dreaming of. The only bloody thing that has changed in all this time is that I'm in the best shape of my life. But really…big whoop!'

And then I stopped.

You could have heard a pin drop in my mind.

Radio silence.

Crickets.

The reality of that statement slammed down on me at full force.

Yes, I am in better shape. And working-out is the only

thing I have committed to day in and day out, week in and week out, month in and month out.

Everything else?

I've done everything else exactly according to my Broken Recipe. I've done this a bit, then that a bit, then stopped (hey, life happens). Then I bounced to the next thing (ooh, look at that bright and shiny new thing!). Then I stopped again (summer vacation). Then I found the program to beat all programs (and didn't finish it because I found another program that *really* was the program). Then I realized it wasn't really the program after all (hey, that happens, too). And then came the holidays (and that's legit — no one sticks to anything during the holidays).

You see where this is going.

On.

And on.

And on it went.

Broken Recipe all the way.

But working out?

Here's how that went down: I signed up. I showed up. I showed up again. And again. And again. Days off? Yes. Weeks off? Yup. (Life happens, right?) But then I went right back to it. Each and every time. I stayed with it, for the long-haul.

Can you guess what happened?

I got in shape.

Of course I did.

The Way = Practice.

You would think the concept of "showing up
regularly and experiencing success as a result" would
not qualify as 'Aha!' material—but I'm so totally
human it can be ridiculous.

Does this ring any bells for you?

I believe in my heart that there are millions (billions?)
of us out there with the noblest of intentions. We want
something better in our lives—for ourselves and for
our loved ones. And we do our best to make changes
in that direction.

But somewhere along the way, we falter. We fail to
stick with it and see it through.

There are as many reasons for this as there are
dreams. Every single one of those reasons is valid.
Every single time you stopped, or got distracted, or
gave up, or failed—every one of those moments and
reasons is real and okay.

It's time to love these moments—allow them to be

what they are, and then let go of them. Do not let them hold power over you any longer as failures. Do not spend another second beating yourself up over them. That does nothing but hold you back even more. It is time to move on.

Looking In:

What did you think of that working out story? How did you find yourself reacting? Were you thinking, 'Duh!' or, 'Wow, when she puts it that way...' or something in between? It's valuable to note your reaction, to see where you're at in all of this, and to see where your own falterings have been. The more honest we can be with ourselves, the faster we move forward.

Grab your journal and let's get to it. Remember, answer the questions as if you were a young kid. No holds barred, stream of consciousness. No judgement. Write it all down.

1. If you were guaranteed that you could not fail, what changes would you want to bring into your life? List 10 of them, and keep going until you've got nothing left. Don't be bashful—have a grand, playful time here!

2. Now, choose one of these changes, goals or outcomes. Imagine a year

or two into the future, and you
have achieved the goal. Close your
eyes for a moment, and be in the
space of this New You.

Digging Deeper:

Now that you're in this space of possibility, it's time
to write a letter from Future You—this expanded,
happier, more abundant version of You—back in time
to Current You.

You may have done this exercise before, and if that's
the case, please just hop in and do it again. Why?
Because you are a different person now than you
were the last time you wrote it. And also because each
time you drop into this space, each time you tap into
that future you, you are creating from a sacred place.
It is part of the process. (Really. Trust me!)

1. Start with, "Dearest..." to show the
    amount of respect and love and
    gratitude that Future You feels
    toward Current You.

2. Describe what life is like for this
    New You. How do you feel each
    morning? Each night? What is
    different now? What is it like to be
    on the other side of the changes
    you've made. See and feel in as

much detail as possible, and enjoy
the peace and joy.

This is your gold—make it shine!

This is the heart of why you desire the changes in the
first place. Savor the feelings, and let them seep into
your cells. Absorb the goodness.

3. Now, encourage the Current You.
Let her know that everything she
needs is already within her.
Mention specific qualities that can
help see her through to success. Be
generous and loving, as you see
her from this wiser, compassionate
perspective.

4. Express your sincere gratitude to
Current You for all that she is
putting into these changes. The
Universe LOVES gratitude — and
your soul does, too.

5. Add anything else that Future You
wants to convey to Current You.
Fill your letter with perspective,
knowing, love, and admiration.

This letter, these feelings, they are your gold. They're
what drive you, and it's important to keep them close
by, at the forefront of your mind. Because your
breakthrough will come only when your gold

(enthusiasm, commitment, desire, fire, yearning, and sometimes even need) are big and bright enough to outweigh any resistance that has been holding you back from becoming that New You.

An Old Fashioned Balance-scale

Here's one way of looking at that last statement.

Imagine an old-fashioned scale. Currently, and perhaps for years, the right side of your scale has been weighed down quite a bit. These are the *shoulds*, the *shouldn'ts*, the to-dos, the chores, tasks, scout meetings, the 'I don't have time,' 'I don't have money,' and every other manner of excuse or block that has prevented you from living your dreams. To date, they have been outweighing your gold, and this is why you aren't right smack dab where you want to be.

Your gold, on the other hand, is what rests gloriously on the left side of the scale. When the scale finally tips in that direction—and not a moment sooner—you will have your breakthrough.

This is why it is so valuable to visit your gold daily. Take it out, admire it, try it on for size as if it were a fabulously blingy ring, or a quietly-sophisticated watch, or whatever suits your fancy. Play with this gold. Re-read your letter from Future You. Breathe into the feeling you have as you envision that you've already made this change. Feel how light, powerful, expansive, peaceful, confident, and grateful you are. Shine this light!

Can you feel the scale tipping to the left?

Our job here is to tip it as much as we can.

Remember how I said I wasn't just going to tell you about the secret to manifestation, but that I would also guide you toward real success? That's what we're doing here, so stay with me.

Given that our goal is to tip the old-fashioned balance-scale to the left as much as possible, the other half of our strategy is to lighten up the right side of the scale.

This is more difficult for most people, so if you just felt a tightening or sense of dread, know that you're not alone.

The joy of adding gold is much more exciting (and sexy!) than releasing the '*shoulds.*' Unburdening the left-hand side of the scale like this often feels, at least at first, like we're letting people down, backing out of commitments, slacking, or even failing. This part of the process often takes courage and a whole lot of commitment-to-self. It requires change, and even slight change can be frightening.

We're going to take a closer look at the right side of your scale in the next chapter. For now, rest assured that you're not going to make major changes all at once. In fact, I strongly recommend that you don't, unless you've already thought long and hard, from all different angles, and know that you are at the tipping point of bringing glorious, big change into your life. And if that's the case, remember to stay grounded to your heart-center as you move forward.

For most of us, though, small changes— or what I like to call Baby Steps—are the most s   ption. Baby Steps allow you to adjust   or those around you to get acc   nges, instead of being jarred by   stant to) major upheavals.

CHAPTER SEVEN

Letting Go of Too Much

> *In order to experience the light*
> *side of anything one must also*
> *admire the differing shades of grey,*
> *for it is in those dark spaces we*
> *find faith lying in wait to envelop*
> *us.*

There's a little story I often find myself sharing with my clients, in order to help them say "no" to things.

Imagine you have to be the bake sale Chairwoman, yet again, because you are every year, and there's no one else who can do it—or so you think (has anyone guessed yet that I love baking?). But unbeknownst to you, there's another person—we'll call him Sam— who is eager to step into a role in the community, and bake sale Chairman is right up his alley. Sam plans to volunteer for the job, until he finds out that the same person — you — is Chair again this year. Alas, Sam stays in the shadows, not as involved as he wants to be and not able to fill his potential. Meanwhile, you grudgingly fulfill the role and it leaves you spread thin, once again.

I've had my own experiences like this. Not long ago I was asked to be the Booster Club Chair for one of my son's baseball teams. I was flattered and I feel strongly about supporting the team. Yes, this is true... and... I also knew it wasn't a good fit for me.

Why?

Because my plate was already full to overflowing. I was writing a book, launching a podcast, we'd just gotten a puppy, my husband and I were both traveling a ton, the list went on and on. I could feel the tightness inside me, as well as an army of *shoulds* that were already launching a private assault.

Now here's the thing. I could have let the *shoulds* win. Those voices were loud, insistent and full of judgment. But at this point I know enough about those darned *shoulds* to realize they are wrapped up in ego instead of genuine service. So I dug deep and told the coach I would be happy to help in other ways, but that I simply wasn't the right person to coordinate the whole thing.

Did I feel badly? Of course I did! But I also know that over-extending ourselves often leads to frustration, stress, and resentment. In the end, two other moms stepped up to co-chair, and they have been doing an incredible job with it—far better than I would have been able to do.

(If that story stung you as "selfish!" please rest assured that you're not the only one who has that initial reaction to this very deeply-entrenched belief system of "do, do, do—for others!" I get into it more in just a bit, but it is an important perspective shift that I'd be honored to help you make. Life becomes vastly more expansive when we come to understand the value of also "doing" for ourselves, which is often as easy to do as simply saying no.)

See, we can't possibly know all that the Universe has in its plans for us or for those around us. When we think otherwise, we feel compelled to "solve" everything (e.g. listening to the *shoulds* even when another part of us is telling us something different). When that happens, we very likely are robbing ourselves—and others—of an opportunity.

That's not to say it's good to be a slacker and let everything go, but rather that there's great value when we practice saying yes to what feels expansive, and saying no to the *shoulds* a little more often. This is when we truly let the Universe work its infinite magic.

Surely, the Universe knows what it's doing. The best we can do is what's truly, deeply best for us, and then let it go and allow the rest of it play out as it's meant to.

This concept can help reduce the sting of otherwise painful situations. I'll give you another example, based on a job I applied for a while back. I was in a lack-of-faith slump about my business, and I had a really wonderful job opportunity come across my desk. It seemed sent from the heavens—a chance to work for and learn from someone I'd admired for quite some time, while also continuing to grow my company on the side. I applied, knowing that I would bring an extraordinary amount to the job—not just the technical side of what they were after, but the amazing, inspiring energy that I knew would benefit them greatly.

I waited excitedly to hear back from them.

And I waited.

And I waited some more.

You can guess the punchline: I didn't get the job.

I was kind of heartbroken, because I'd really seen it as a great solution to so much I wanted to create in my life. But thankfully, I also know the truth of this concept we just discussed: we simply don't know all the parts that are in motion. We can't presume to know the game plan, let alone be the constant director of it. The puzzle is too intricate and interconnected, and our human minds are simply not sophisticated enough to see it in its entirety.

In this light, it was pretty easy to let the disappointment go, literally, with the thought, "Okay, that must mean something better is on its way."

And it was.

My business began to experience tremendous growth—you know, that business I would have let slide if I'd been offered the job. Frankly, I'm pretty certain this book wouldn't have been written either. When you think about it, maybe you are the reason I didn't get the job! Perhaps you needed this book, these lessons, these changes that are happening inside of you.

(And for the record, if it was you who manifested me writing this book instead of getting that job, this is me sending a big, hearty thank you your way!)

The inner workings of this infinitely benevolent Universe are too complicated for us to ever really know why things work out the way they do. But we can have faith that they're working out for our highest and best.

And we allow it free reign to do so when we listen to the whispers it's sending us—that feeling in the pit of our stomach about taking on a certain task, the hesitation we feel about something else. These are all messages, and the more we listen, the more we get out of the way and let the Universe do its thing!

We are not meant to be the choreographers of the world, but rather of our own highest good. From there, we release and let Source do the rest.

So, are you ready?

Looking In:

1. List your current obligations that take mental, physical and emotional energy out of you. In other words, where do you put your time each day? What drains you even when you are not actively "doing" it? What else? Write it all down.

2. Put a star next to the items that are non-negotiable—those commitments that you simply can't dial back, or drop, or those emotional attachments that you know you can't let go of right now. [Note that someday you might be able to let these things go, but for now, we're focusing on Baby Steps.]

3. On a new page, re-write the list,
    this time only including the ones
    that you possibly can let go of. If it
    helps you to rank them in order of
    how easy they will be to release,
    go ahead and do that. Or just put a
    check mark next to the easiest
    ones. These are the "too much"
    that you're going to begin letting
    go of.

The purpose of this exercise is to take full, honest
stock of those things that are holding you back from
pursuing your dreams. Most of us don't even realize
the huge number of things that we give—often
unconsciously—our energy to.

In other words, it's likely that you're so remarkably
busy with all the things you do—work, parenting,
keeping up with the house, volunteering at your kids'
schools, taking care of your aging parents—that your
own personal goals (and following through with
them) are not consistently prioritized in your daily
tasks.

*They might be the utmost priority in your mind, but
they get buried underneath all the other tasks on your
daily to-do list.*

While it is most certainly important to keep up some
specific commitments, in the end, the most important
commitments we can keep are the ones we make to
ourselves.

I know that's a tough pill for many people to swallow. I get it. We have been brought up to believe the exact opposite. I want to plant this seed though, because self-commitment is ultimately the seed to beat all seeds.

More on that later. For now, let's return to our Baby Steps.

Digging Deeper:

From the list you made in Looking In Question #3, choose 1-2 items that you are comfortable "releasing" in the next week. Perhaps you can delegate these tasks. Perhaps it's time to graciously step down from a committee. Alternatively, you could pledge not to volunteer the next time you are asked to. The important part is to decide how/when you will cut back on a couple non-essential commitments.

Write them down. Put them in your schedule, if appropriate. This process of writing will help you stay accountable. At the very least, schedule a reminder for 3 days from now, to check in on your progress.

This "saying no" is a big deal to a lot of people. It's tough, it rubs them the wrong way, it smells of selfishness, or they think it's just plain wrong. At the same time, there's something deep inside of them that resonates with it nonetheless. It might be just a silent knowing, but it's there.

It's there because the higher parts of us knows how true it is—that when we ourselves are filled, then we have more to give to those around us.

The art of saying "no" is a critical practice in and of itself. If we are filled-to-overflowing with commitments to others, it is impossible to commit to ourselves, which means our dreams don't stand a chance.

We simply must clear space—even just a little—if we are to have the time, and more importantly our energy, to what we are setting forth to do.

CHAPTER EIGHT

Why Practice Matters So Very Much

*Self-imposed boundaries are often
the hardest to maintain, but they
yield the most abundant fruit.*

Let's pause for a moment and consider what you've accomplished so far. If you're thinking it doesn't seem like much, rest assured—you've done some serious work.

You've got energy moving and bubbling around your goals and dreams. In doing so, you added weight to the left-side of the balance scale: your gold. You also took an honest look at what you're currently prioritizing above your own goals and dreams, and began the work of lightening the right side of the scale. You started taking action to super-size your commitment to your gold. And you took real-life steps to free up some time and energy, in order to create space to focus on actually making your dreams a reality.

This is the same path that my client Charles took with me a couple years back. Charles sought me out because he knew something had to change in order to achieve his dreams and goals. He'd long been aware of law of attraction and had been, to a certain extent, an active participant in the creation of his life. He was very receptive to energy work, which is why he knew we'd be such a terrific fit.

At the time he came to me for coaching, Charles was a year and a half into a high-powered, prominent job that wasn't going at all as he'd hoped. The stress was taking a major on him. He also wanted to be in better control of his financial future, and have a partner to share his life with—no easy task in the small town in which he lived.

We spent a lot of our time together digging deep into the specific aspects—and energies—that weren't working in his current job, as well as dreaming up ideal outcomes that in most cases weren't related to his current reality. We applied this latter approach—of going into sacred space to imagine and invite magical, unforeseen possibilities—to his love life as well.

For his part, Charles practiced diligently a type of allowing that was foreign to him; he consistently "allowed" that situations could unexpectedly change, and he "allowed" that he didn't need to tightly manage and control every aspect of every situation. He was a stellar student, and a great example of what happens when one goes all-in on their commitment to their Practice.

In the end, Charles left the job, from a place of deep inner power. He had exhausted all reasonable options - of being willing to take all steps that were aligned with him, but no longer willing to take the ones that were running him into the ground and were not ever going to change. He was able to move on knowing he'd done the best he could to make things work. It simply wasn't the right position for him, and he wasn't going to settle.

As he opened his energy in this way, the Universe "magically" shifted around those other puzzle pieces as well.

He found that, with just a little planning, he had a financial cushion that enabled him to feel secure and take his time in the search for a new, just-right job.

And as I write this, Charles just celebrated his first anniversary with a man he describes as, *"exactly what I was looking for…Things clicked so fast, it's hard to describe it as anything other than love at first sight. Explain it however it makes your brain comfortable— either the energy work I was doing made me more open to going out and meeting people, and I met someone… or perhaps the thoughts I sent out to the universe were manifested in the best possible person*

*and relationship I could imagine. I can hold the
cognitive dissonance of both ideas comfortably in my
mind and just be grateful to have him in my life.
Thank you, universe!"*

Having coached Charles through implementing the
changes that changed his life, I don't believe it is any
accident that he has found himself very much in the
place he hoped to be, and well on his way to still
better things.

While you and I haven't had the chance to coach
privately, I have already walked you through many of
the power-building processes that Charles and I
worked through together. That's the beauty of this
book! And whether you feel it or not (although I
suspect you do), they've begun to create a whole lot
of movement—at least energetically, and perhaps
already in the physical world. Congratulations!

The Value of Drilling

Now that you've set these changes in motion, let's
take a bit of time to look more closely at how and
why The Power of Practice is so magical. We're
doing this in order to begin filling those newly-
emptied spaces with a sparkling light—with the
vibration of possibility, divine support and guidance.

Why does that matter? First, because when you let go
of old patterns, it's important to fill the freshly-
cleared space with something new (otherwise those

newly-emptied spaces will, by default, fill back up with the old ways). Second, because it's another way of adding weight to the left side of your scale. Every step you take in an empowered, expanded directions puts more gold there. Simply reading this book is adding to it. And as we add more and more, we finally tip that scale for good.

Let's begin by conjuring up an image of a major league baseball player. I once heard that the good ones hit 1,000 balls every single day of training. Surely they "already know" how to hit a ball. Why keep such a grueling practice schedule then? Because they know that it's this persistent drilling that makes them a Master.

A little closer to home, and a lot less major-league, I was a starter on my school's JV basketball team in ninth grade, and by my sophomore year I was playing Varsity. That's big doings in a lot of ways, but of course there was room for growth. For one thing, it became clear that I was greatly lacking in the left-handed layup department.

The problem was that my left hand refused to cooperate. The solution was to get it so accustomed to the motion that there was no cooperation involved— but rather it just did what it knew to do. Cellular re-patterning, that's what I was up to. I must have spent 20 or 30 hours—before practice, after practice, and on weekends—just putting that ball up, again and again, with my uncoordinated left hand.

Magic eventually happened, and the day soon came when I could hit every left-handed layup I tried. I still can (well, maybe not *every* one). I can't throw a baseball, football, or anything else with that foolish left hand, but I ingrained that one little flick-of-the-wrist layup shot, and it is here to stay.

This is what we're talking about, when we talk about Practice.

Staying with something long enough that it becomes part of us, ingrained. Practicing something so diligently that it launches us past the hobby stage and into the realm of the expert.

Practice = Discipline = Perseverance = Commitment = Sticking With It

I could have called this book Discipline. Or Perseverance. Or Commitment. Or Sticking-With-It.

I chose to call it Practice.

I did this largely because in my mind it's the softest of the terms. And I know that there are many of you out there who, like me, have some level of resistance to "discipline." By softening the term—as well as the approach—my goal is to reach all the people who, like myself, have been resisting for too long.

The problem with this resistance, of course, is that it's only been serving to hold us back. Our disdain for the concept of discipline has caused us to remain novices—at the expense of the things we most want to create in our lives. Once we cease to resist, and instead allow for the immense value of practice, we finally can become the masters that we've been longing to be.

The other reason I chose the word 'practice' is that it was practice that has brought us all our current successes. Think for a moment: was it not through practice that each of us became proficient at walking, talking, reading, tying our shoes, riding a bike, or downshifting a manual car while taking a left turn and tuning the radio station all at the same time?

I dare say none of these would have happened if we'd only put in a few attempts, or moved on to the next thing before we succeeded in learning each of these.

It is through practice that we run the marathon, learn to play Hendrix, change a diaper in 10 seconds, become proficient artists dancers skateboarders surfers public-speakers mechanics computer-programmers meditators you-get-the-picture. It is even through practice that we learn to be happy.

Every single one of these is something that we were once terrible at (except for the happiness piece—we were all masters at that when we were young), but through the sheer art of practice, we got better.

Our goals and dreams are no different. They are constructed of the same material: desire. So just as we did when we learned to walk, we must practice our goal frequently, consistently, without giving up, until it is ingrained in our fiber. That's how we achieve success in whatever we choose to manifest—whether it be happiness, abundance, health or anything else our hearts and minds desire.

I once heard Wayne Dyer speak about his running, and he said something to the effect of, "I have run 10 miles a day, every day, for the past 15 years. I have not missed a single day."

I was stunned—nothing short of flabbergasted—when I heard this (and I'm 99% certain I heard it correctly). Who on earth is that disciplined about anything? I'm not even that solid with brushing my teeth or changing my socks!

"Who does that?" I wondered.

And then I realized: *Wayne Dyer does that—that's who.*

Someone who published 40 books in as many years, that's who. Someone with a phenomenal, best-selling career. Someone who has changed the lives of millions for the better. That's who.

It takes a real commitment to create the life of our dreams. It won't happen with a passing fancy, or two weeks of affirmations. Trust me, I've tried that approach. By the same token, we can't manifest something new if we bounce from one practice to the next, just like we couldn't have mastered the stick-shift if we decided to take the bus instead. It simply doesn't work that way.

CHAPTER NINE

Digging a New Groove

*The interconnectedness of the
Universe only allows for success
for all of us.*

The Universe is built for success. It is set up for
infinite abundance. Your dream may be financial
abundance, health, love, joy, or anything under the
sun. Whatever it is, Source energy is conspiring in
your favor, to bring those very things into your
experience.

Why then, are some people successful at these things,
and others seem not to be?

The successful show up, day and in day out. Whether
this means maintaining a successful meditation
practice, or successfully getting sober, or creating

financial success—it is something they do day after day after day after day.

Yes, this is about commitment, as we discussed in the last chapter.

But it's also about actually doing the Practice. Not just feeling committed to it, but actually taking action.

The successful show up when it rains, and when there's a drought. They show up when there's a snow storm, and when it's a perfect day at the beach. They show up when they're sick, and when their daughter is getting married (okay, maybe not this one). They are successful because they show up, consistently.

Without showing up consistently, over a long stretch of time, we simply cannot create a new path in our lives. Why?

Because we are not doing enough to rewire our old patterns.

I like to think of these habits, or entrenched patterns, as grooves. In fact, I've dubbed it my Brain Groove Theory (although I suspect researchers have a more science-y term for it).

Here how it goes. Imagine a habit you want to change—maybe you want to go from people-pleasing to standing up for yourself, or from not-exercising to working out two times per week. Or maybe you just want to have a more positive, can-do attitude in life.

Picture your current habit (e.g. people-pleasing) as a deep groove, like a path that's been dug by the side of the road, over and over and over again, until it's a trench.

Typically, when we're unconscious of our habits, we're down in that groove or trench. We've grown accustomed to being there. We know the view, and it's what we expect. Nothing changes—we just go about our business as usual. Even if it's not what we really want, it's comfortable enough because it's familiar.

In order to make any real change, we must first somehow decide we're going to make that change happen. Once we do—once we decide we don't want to be in that particular trench anymore—we are instantly catapulted up to road-level. And we now have an entirely new view of the terrain—of our life, specifically, of what it can be and what we want it to be.

This is a beautiful, inspiring, motivating expanse of potentiality that we now can see. It feels new, and different, and better. We feel free!

So what do we do? We excitedly start digging a new trench for our "change." We start doing this new thing. We are working toward our goal and it feels great! It's exactly what we're meant to be doing. Dig that trench. Dig it today, and tomorrow, and the next. Keep going into next week and next month. Don't stop—whatever you do, don't stop! I know it's

raining today, but keep digging. I know it's hot this
month, but please, keep digging! You need a week
off? Okay, that's cool, as long as you get right back to
digging this same trench.

Here's the key: you've got to stick with that new
trench (habit, pattern, path), and you've got to keep
on digging until it's deep enough, so that when things
get wobbly (as they invariably do), you don't fall
back into the old one.

Only when your new groove is deep enough will you
finally escape the gravitational pull of falling back
into the old groove.

There's a saying I heard years ago that has always
stuck with me. It was, "awareness is instantaneous;
change is glacial."

While I don't believe this to be an absolute truth, it
does seem to be how life works for most of us, most
of the time. We suddenly and joyfully decide upon a
new way we want to be, and it's an inspired, exciting
feeling. We are motivated into action. For a bit
anyway.

Here's the thing: that's the easy part. It's when the
original thrill wears off that the real work begins. This
is not sexy, I get it. That's the entire point. If we only
stick with the sexiness of the thrill, then we don't
stick with digging the new groove. And the actual
change only comes in the weeks and months (and
sometimes years) of taking action.

I want to offer another visual, one that speaks to the dangerous nature of old habits creeping back in, before we have the chance to fully establish the new ones.

Imagine you're building a cabin in the jungle. You start clearing the plot of land. Given the crazy speed of vegetation growth in the tropics, the vines and weeds are seemingly unstoppable. They constantly encroach on your project. You won't ever get the whole lot cleared, and the cabin built, if you proceed in an on-again, off-again manner. But if you stick with the clearing, day after day, and stay ahead of the new growth, then you'll have the chance to build a beautiful wall to hold back the weeds. You'll have your home built soon thereafter, and at that point all it will take is general maintenance.

The same holds true with your goals and dreams. They need the same consistency and commitment as your land-clearing, wall-making, and hut-building. Without such diligence, they too will be encroached upon—by the other demands that are always waiting in the shadows to take over.

Looking In:

Before we move on, let's take a look at how you typically dig grooves or clear land. What has been your pattern up to now, when you set off on a new goal, or to create a new habit?

Go ahead and grab your notebook.

1. When you set a goal, or commit to a change, how long do you usually stick with it? One week? Three? Until it is completely incorporated into your life? Until something comes up? Until you get bored with it and move on? Take a deeply honest look at how things have gone down in the past.

2. What type of results do you typically see when you set a goal for yourself?

3. How do you feel while you're sticking with it?

4. If you tend to get derailed or distracted, what typically derails/distracts you?

5. How do you feel once derailed/distracted?

6. Do you go back to it, or pick up something else?

7. How long does it take you before you start up again? Or do you move straight on to the next thing?

As much as you might not like what you find, it's still really helpful to take an honest look at your process. Only then will you have a real sense of how you currently approach your goals. You will see the patterns that currently have a hold on you—the patterns that have been holding you back from getting to your goals and dreams.

Once you see them, you can create new strategies to work around them. And more importantly, by bringing those old patterns into the light, you shift the power dynamics around them. Instead of your old patterns having control over you—by habit or fear— you instead take the first step in reclaiming control of your choices and actions.

So let's do this:

We're going to take it a step further, to jostle these old patterns out of their stuck places. Again, when we move energy like this, we are loosening it so that we can release it. Because if that old-pattern-energy still has its teeth in you, it's really, really tough to carve your new groove.

Digging Deeper:

It's time to have a compassionate talk with these old patterns—also known as your current habits. You can copy the words below (if you do, make sure to let them sink in) or write your own words. The key is to express your gratitude for what these stop/start or other patterns have done for you in the past, send them on their way, and claim your new way of being.

Remember, the more you dive into the place of communing with the energy that you're speaking to in these exercises, the more powerful the shifts you will experience.

Why would you want to be compassionate with those aspects that have wronged you?

Because the truth is, those patterns have actually been supporting you in countless ways—even if you cannot currently see that. They are strategies that you created at some point—most likely in childhood—that have long served to protect us. As such, we honor and thank them. Yes, we are asking them to leave, or to transform into something new, but we never want to push at them or be angry with them. To do that would be to attack a part of ourselves, and this never serves. Instead, we acknowledge them, love them, and tell them we no longer need them to play the part that they've been playing.

Note: *In case you're hesitating on this exercise for any reason, I want to highly encourage you to do it, and to give yourself into it as much as possible. This is a piece of one of the most powerful techniques I use with my private clients. It is adapted from a process developed by my amazing coaching school, the Institute for Professional Excellence in Coaching, and shared here with their permission.*

1. "I see you, old patterns that (in the past) have kept me from my dreams. ____ is what I do when you are in charge."

2. "I appreciate all that you may have done for me in the past, but you are no longer serving me in a helpful way. So I'm choosing to let you go (or asking you to take on a new role—whichever feels better to you)."

3. "I know you may be comfortable, because you're familiar. And perhaps you've kept me from some embarrassing situations or perceived-failures in the past. Thank you for that. But now I am growing into a new place, I am becoming a new me. And I am choosing new patterns, new beliefs, and new ways of being."

4. "So I invite you to leave now, or to do a new job." (You can dialogue with this energy—really, do it—to see what new job it can do to help you, rather than hold you back).

5. Write anything else to say to these old patterns, as you bless them and let them go. Be kind and gentle

with yourself, and with the old
patterns that you are releasing or
transforming.

Good work!

Brilliant.

Another big chunk of no-longer-serving-you energy
has just been looked at, honored, and released or
alchemized.

This is a good time to remind you to take extra good
care of yourself while you go through this book.
Moving big energy can be intense. Our bodies
sometimes react with fatigue or sickness, our hearts
often feel more vulnerable, and we may get resistance
from those around us (even our friends and loved
ones).

Remember that this is all part of making changes in
your life, and in fact these uncomfortable side-effects
may have been your "stopping point" in the past—
they could well have been the very thing that halted
your progress. I encourage you to view them not as
stop signs, but instead as sign posts, signaling you're
on a powerful path to finally achieving your dream or
goal. I know it's not easy. This is when self-care,
sleep, exercise, healthy eating, and self-love become
more important than ever.

CHAPTER TEN

The Curse of Imperfections

*When in need of assistance, all one
has to do is ask and guides will
appear to assist in creating your
highest and best.*

I'm going to hazard a guess about you. I'm going to
guess that you are very deeply committed to your
dreams.

I'm also going to guess that you aren't afraid of hard
work. And that, in fact, you've been working really
hard—perhaps for a long time—to make your dreams
come true. You've summoned big courage at times,
and licked a lot of wounds at other times. But every
single time you've missed your mark, you've gone
back out there to try again.

Am I right?

Let's pause for a moment, and take a look at the beauty of this from an outside perspective. There's a little game I like to play—with myself and with my clients—and I want to teach it to you.

When I know it's time for a surge of compassionate, heart-based perspective, I imagine I'm sitting on the moon, hanging out with my Higher Self. We sit there side by side, admiring "me" down on earth. We notice the courage she pulls up, day in and day out, always daring to get out there and give it another shot. We are amazed by her tenacity, and inspired by her determination. So many times, she could have quit—it would have been far easier to do that than to summon up another wave of commitment. And yet there she is, still finding the strength to face her fears, tap into her faith, and open her heart.

When you look at it this way, it's easy to see how truly awesome you are. I know you might not always feel it in your day-to-day life. I get it. But the truth is, you are powerful, and you do have what it takes. Otherwise you wouldn't still be pursuing your dreams.

Dissolving More Things Blocking Our Path

I believe what I just said:

You are powerful.

And I believe you know it, too. Somewhere deep inside you is a voice - maybe just a whisper or a knowing - that reminds you of the infinite, beautiful source of power that you are.

And while this is wholly true, I've seen time and again how even the most capable of us still unconsciously hold ourselves back.

We are not wrong or bad for doing this—there is no wrong, from the cosmic, divine perspective of things. We are simply being given an opportunity for growth. And our growth can occur right here, right now, as we take just a little bit of time for an honest look at those things we unconsciously do to stunt our magnificence.

What are these things?

First and foremost, they're things that we can choose to keep holding onto, or we can choose to let them go. They are the blocks that have been holding us back. We've already talked about some of them. We're going to be dealing with the others now.

Here's something that you may or may not have figured out about me: I always view things from an energetic perspective.

Remember the old-fashioned balance-scale, with all the *shoulds* and to-do's on the right, and your dreams, inspiration, courage, and commitment on the left?

From my lens, everything on the right side of the scale is actually draining your energetic systems. Your power is literally being seeped into these blocks. And when we leak energy to our blocks—when we let them control us through our fears and worries—we lose the power and strength to move forward into our dreams.

On the flip side, when we find a way to release or dissolve these blocks—by looking at them with courage and honesty, and then actively releasing them—we make magic happen. This is what we did with the "letting go of too much" exercise, as well as when we changed the old stop/start patterns by digging a new groove. We effectively took away the power they once had over us.

It's like putting a plug into an energetic black hole. Our power stays with us, instead of being sucked into our blocks. And that leaves us with a whole lot more power with which to achieve our dreams.

Don't worry - it will be easy, and perhaps even enjoyable! We don't need to dig deep into the history or roots of our blocks. In fact, sometimes when we start digging too deep, we stunt our forward movement because we can get stuck in a cycle of tracing or re-living their origin.

That said, if you know that your blocks are deep, and you feel you're ready to unravel them, then now may be a great time for you to go do that deeper work. This is especially true if you are aware of a trauma. If that's the case for you right now, I honor you for recognizing it, and strongly encourage you to seek help from a professional who is a supportive fit for you. Whatever you are facing can be worked through with the guidance of a trained therapist.

When our blocks are basic and more simplistic (old patterns, habits, beliefs), we can move mountains just by naming them, getting to know them, and sending them on their way—as we did when we wrote a letter to our old patterns. It's like shining a flashlight on the monster in the closet: it's nowhere near as scary once the lights are on. In fact, sometimes it's not even there anymore.

So, let's get keep going and clear more blocks! We're going to take a look at some of the more common ones and do a couple of simple exercises to dissolve them.

Imprefections

We'll start with the heavy-hitter. We all have this fear—that of imperfection—to some degree or another. If you ever meet someone who doesn't have it, they're either a Zen monk, or they're covering up their imperfections because they're afraid of being imperfect!

So we spend all this time holding ourselves back, because we fear we won't be "good enough" at whatever we're wanting to do. We wait until we feel like we're ready, until we'll do it right, until we're perfect.

But here's the catch.

Nobody's. Perfect. Ever.

It is true. Nobody is perfect. Not even the perfect people.

[**Note:** Did you catch my typo up above? I misspelled the header "Imprefections" on purpose. Actually, it was an accident in the first draft, but I loved the "nod" it gave in the direction of allowing imperfections, and wanted to keep it in the final. So there it is, an officially misspelled title in a fabulous book. Imperfect, and perfectly fine nonetheless.]

If you look at it, we all have weak points. Every single one of us. They are all different. My weak spots are different from yours. Yours are different from the next person's.

Often we think our weaknesses are bad. Okay, we almost always think they're bad. We were taught to believe that. I mean, they're weaknesses. Who wants to be weak? No one, right?

So we work hard to hide our weaknesses, or fight them, or drown them in addictions, or bulldoze them by being over-achievers or workaholics. The trouble with this is that we spend our energy dodging or covering up our weaknesses, and then have no time or energy to move forward.

If we look deeper at this, we see that it's a double-edged sword. Not only are we draining our precious and divine energy, we're actually giving it to something that in turn holds us back even more! We are tending to something that holds us down, thinking, "as soon as I am free of this, then all will be fine." And often we simply spin our wheels on imperfection after imperfection. We waste our time and energy staying afloat, instead of using that energy to carry us forward to where we want to be.

In order to move into a new version of ourselves, we must:

1. Make the conscious choice to release the tight hold we have on our imperfections.

2. Choose to accept these imperfect aspects as part of the whole package that is "me."

3. Put our precious and powerful energy into actively creating our new self, not into fixing perceived imperfections.

Notice through all of this, we are allowing that these imperfections exist.

We're not denying them. We're not pushing them
away or hating them. Instead, we're recognizing
them, acknowledging them, allowing them to be.
Perhaps we can even give them some Love. But
above all else, we are choosing to no longer get stuck
on them—to no longer give them our power.

As a way of getting to know, and then move past,
your own "imperfection-based" energy-drains, see if
you recognize any of these. Have they held you back
from moving forward toward your goals or dreams?

1. I am sorting through my "stuff."

"When I'm all done sorting through my 'stuff,' I will
finally be able to achieve the life of my dreams."

And by 'stuff' we mean wounds, scars, things that
seem to have us not being the confident, happy self
we want to be. Maybe it was divorce; a tough
childhood; being told you were stupid; being laughed
at you when you were onstage; your dad leaving you;
your parents teaching you money is evil; being told
you'd never amount to anything; being ignored in
junior high or teased in high school; a combination of
any of these and more.

Honestly, I get it.

There is so much value in healing oneself. Every
single one of us has blocks or trauma, or a series of
them, that get in the way of feeling ready or worthy.

But here's the thing. We can't turn back the clock and undo these events. Nor does it work to leave them alone, pretend they don't exist, or stuff them down inside of us. Sometimes a good therapist is needed, but other times some basic energy work will do the trick.

For starters, you can simply practice "loving you" right now, exactly where you are.

Take a minute now to love that young child, the one who remains inside of you at this very moment. Embrace that little one—even if it's your very first time doing so—and let her know you see her. Talk to her –let her know you appreciate all she went through, all the walls she built up to protect you, all the hardships she has made it through. If it feels right, write her a letter, sharing all of these things. Honor that little one, and let her know how deeply you love and admire her.

Do not wait, however, until you feel fully at peace, completely healed, or totally Zen to get real about creating the life of your dreams. That is a life-long journey, and it is likely that your Practice—the act of you moving actively toward your dreams—is a powerful step on that journey.

2. I am lacking.

"I don't have enough education—I need more before I can start, let alone achieve, my dreams. I don't have

enough money to do this thing. There is not enough
time in the day for what I have going on—I certainly
don't have any left over for my dreams. I am not
pretty enough, or strong enough, or connected
enough. I am not talented enough. I don't have what it
takes."

Again, I get it. I hear you. I've been there. And the
only thing that puts me where I'm at, instead of where
I used to be, is that I insisted on making those fears
secondary to my commitment. I decided to say,
"Okay, those may or may not be true. Who knows?
But I'm never going to get to where I want to be if I
keep waiting for those things to be resolved."

It is not easy. These fears and feelings of inadequacy
are very, very real. But please, don't let them stop you
anymore. Do not let them get in the way. Do not let
them win. You are far more powerful, beautiful,
talented, educated than you realize.

Understand too that those voices—those fears—do
not speak the truth. They are a scared part of you,
fighting to hold on to what they know, even though
what they know is false or outdated. They are the ego
part of you, and as such, they do not have your
interests in mind. Instead, they're fighting tooth and
nail to keep you where you are, so that their own
safety is secured. Again, it's critical to love and
accept those parts of you, but it's even more
important not to let them be your master.

3. It's not ready.

"I'm almost ready to launch—it's just not quite there yet…"

This is when we have get stuck in the land of "I really need it to be a bit better before I put it out there." You know, the webpage that just needs a bit more tweaking, the body that will be ready for the gym once it sheds 5 more pounds, the desk and filing system that need a little more organizing, the manuscript, video, workshop that are almost ready to see the light of day, but just need a few final edits.

If you recognize any of these, take a moment to see that you might be sabotaging yourself in the name of perfection.

I like to think about a band's first album. The members of the band continue to play those songs, year after year, even when they themselves have changed dramatically. Perhaps their music has evolved, or they are no longer heartbroken, or they've settled down happily with a wife and kids even though they're still singing their fans' old rowdy, rebellion-fueled favorites. Just think—if they had waited until they were "there," until they had that album perfectly right, the album wouldn't exist; they'd still be waiting to arrive.

We are always changing and growing. There is no end point.

Yes, you might look back at your first workshop or
website, your first workout or meditation and think "I
can't believe I did it when I was that bad." But if you
never did it, you wouldn't be out there improving on
it. You wouldn't be out there birthing your dreams.
You'd be safe and sound, perhaps. You'd be on a
path, yes. And that path would be wonderful in its
own right, because it's the path you're meant to be on
for that stretch of time.

But it wouldn't be the path of turning your dreams
into your reality.

I believe—strike that, I know—you're reading this
because you're on that latter path—the one where you
make it happen. This book found you because your
soul is guiding you into a new version of yourself and
your life. You are being gifted the reminder, the
encouragement, and the support that you've been
asking for.

This is it.

The Universe is responding to your prayers and
intentions. Your soul is helping you step into your
power. You know, deep down, that you are ready to
do this.

Looking In:

Let's take a few minutes now to shift some energy, by
looking at beliefs you may have about why you're not

ready, or not quite able, to create the life of your dreams. Write your responses to each prompt. Write it all out, and when you think you're done with each one, ask yourself "what else?" and write that too.

1. These are all the ways I am not perfect.

2. My biggest fear is that people will discover ____ about me.

3. In order to step powerfully into my dream/goal, I would need ____ to be in place (or out of the picture).

I applaud you, sincerely, for having the courage to dig into these uncomfortable places. It is not easy to dredge up our fears and look our inadequacies squarely in the face. It is, however, extremely powerful in terms taking a good, honest look at what is holding us back.

As before, it's now time to move these fear-based energies out of your system. I'm going to ask you to bless each "imperfection" on your list, by bringing light to it. This is an unconditionally-loving light, a light that has no judgement, and carries a level of love that is far beyond any human-based love you've ever experienced. Once you bless each "imperfection," you will then release it, acknowledging that you no longer want to hold onto that belief about yourself. Here we go.

Digging Deeper:

Write the following for each "imperfection." If it feels right, sit with the sentence for a moment before moving on to the next. Truly feel, see or intend the blessing, and also the invitation for it to leave your energy system.

1. Dear "I am not pretty enough..." I hear you, and I see you, and I know you've been trying to help. I now bless you with this Light, and I release you from my energy patterns.

2. Dear "I am too scared..." I hear you, and I see you, and I know you've been trying to help. I now bless you with this Light, and I release you from my energy patterns.

3. Dear "Others can do it but I can't..."

4. Keep going. Add any other ideas, reasons or excuses that come to mind—anything you can come up with for why you're not yet ready to make your dreams a reality.

This is an incredibly powerful exercise, and I honor you for taking the time to go through it.

It's also a good exercise to do regularly, especially if you're in the midst of feeling particularly stuck or if you've been doubting yourself a lot. Perhaps you want to do it daily, as part of your Practice (it will be easier each time you do it, trust me!). Take note of how you feel after a week or month of blessing and releasing. What has changed for you? Have the "imperfections" loosened up, or even disappeared?

Let's all do what we can to remember that nobody is perfect. In truth, there's not even such a thing as "perfect." So it does no good to wait until things are perfectly lined up and we ourselves are free of our "stuff," because we'll be waiting forever.

Instead, it's up to us to step forward in the midst of feeling imperfect, knowing we are headed in the right direction and that we will continue to correct our course—gently and lovingly—as we move forward.

So how about it—are you ready to commit to "carrying on" even when you feel imperfect? Remember, imperfect action is better than perfect inaction!

CHAPTER ELEVEN

Change

> *When we feel tight, it is a*
> *constriction of our thoughts. It is*
> *an illusion. We are love, therefore*
> *we are infinite.*

In my coaching work, I often find the most successful approach to take with my clients is to begin loosening the outer edges of an issue, rather than tackling it head-on.

I know many coaches ask their clients to plow head-first into their big blocks. And while this might create rapid change, it's been my experience that it doesn't create *lasting* change

Most often, big things are just plain too big. The big blocks are just too blocky.

I have two metaphors for this. Here's the first one: approaching a big block head-on is it a bit like looking directly at the sun—we might try, but in the long run it's just too painful and we eventually we simply have to stop.

On the other hand, if we let the glaring issue stand on its own, and maybe just poke around the edges a little—or even focus on a smaller issue that's much more manageable—then we don't get blinded. Instead, we hop into a success-cycle. We begin to build power and momentum. This is key.

I never take a client into something that is too big for where their power is currently at.

My approach—of building power in this way—is a bit like helping my clients into a pair of sunglasses. The strength that they find in the smaller successes gives them the ability to eventually face the big thing: the sun. And when they do, with this newfound strength (sunglasses), the sun no longer seems so blinding.

Quick note: remember how I mentioned earlier that just knowing that *The Way = Practice* is not enough? That there are other, more important things this book has to offer.

Well, one of the other, major gifts tucked into the book is the step-wise path we've been on. I'm not sure you've noticed, but it's served to help you build up that exact strength.

This is why we're doing all the exercises—so you can actually walk through the steps, get your own momentum fired up, and be ready to tackle the big sun of whatever it is you want to create in your life. Without even realizing it, you've been fitting yourself with a pair of sunglasses.

It's now time to look directly at the sun, which in our case is change. The art of adopting a steady, deliberate practice is, at its core, about making a lasting change in your life.

Let's start with this: change is beautiful.

It's what you're after, right? You want something different in your life. That, by nature, indicates you're after a change.

But while change is indeed desired, there's another angle of change that most of us don't acknowledge quite so directly: change is rarely easy.

In fact, change is most often uncomfortable and sometimes even painful. Even when it's a change we're desperate to make.

Our fear of this discomfort or pain can put a stranglehold on us, even without our realizing it.

Let me tell you a little story. I grew up with a wonderful, loving father who idolized the straight-and-even road. Slow and steady. The fewer bumps, the better. He is a bit of an extreme, with his love—or dare I say worship—of predictability. He is risk-averse, to say the least, which created a wonderfully safe and nurturing environment for his 3 young daughters.

But it did nothing to support my natural tendency to take risks. I was by nature a bit of an outlier in my family in that regard, but I did what was expected of me and dialed back my instinctive spunkiness in order to reduce any waves I might make. To this day my family considers me "impulsive," which is sort of humorous, because to so many others I'm a total play-it-by-the-book type of person.

I say all this with a great deal of love, but the truth is, most of us have been similarly drained of our willingness to take chances and to shake things up. For most of us there's comfort and ease in patterns and predictability. There's control in the known, and a frightening absence of control in the unknown.

Add to this the simple, but major, fact that change takes effort, and you begin to see why we tend to stay where we are. We stay here even if we want something different. Change eats up emotional energy. And it often demands a level of physical energy that most of us feel like we simply don't have.

It's no wonder we resist change, or don't have the strength to create it!

Thoughts like, "I just don't have the time to search for a new job," or, "Where am I going to find the time

in my day to start working out?" are very real for
most of us. We are a tapped out society, on the whole,
so we resort to inaction because it is easier. Staying
where we are is a known quantity, and it doesn't drain
us in the same way that change does.

This is all true.

Yet I'm about to turn that precise assumption on its
head.

Let me ask you: is it really true that it takes less
energy to stay in a lousy situation than it does to
change it? Consider how a sub-par life can suck you
dry, almost imperceptibly, drop by drop. I believe
many of us are numb to such sub-par situations, but
our numbness doesn't mean that it's not taking its toll.

What would happen if we could find a tiny bit more
strength (time, energy) to make a change? What
would happen if we were able to dig just a tiny bit
deeper?

Here's what. It's an illustration that you may recall
from Physics class.

(Wait, come back! It's an easy one, I promise!)

Do you remember the proverbial rock from physics
class, sitting atop a hill, just waiting—yearning,
even—to be rolling down the lush, green hillside?

But it couldn't roll, because it was stuck.

It just sat there, unable to move. That's where so
many of us are at in our current lives. We see the bliss
of rolling down the hill, but we simply can't seem to
get there. We want change, but it's just too big of a
step to take. We don't have the energy, or perhaps the
courage, to make the change happen. We're stuck,
like the rock.

Now, do you remember what the rock needed? It
needed a boost. It had all sorts of potential, but
without the boost, it couldn't get to its happy place.
The boost is the one and only thing that turned its
potential energy (stagnant rock) into kinetic energy
(happily rolling rock).

We are no different.

If you find yourself stuck for fear of change, or fear
of the side-effects the change might have on those
close to you, take heart in this story. When we are
stuck, we are the rock—full of potential, full of desire
for change, but unable to do what it takes to move.

Here again is why this book includes not just
teaching, but also guidance and exercises. It is my
sincere hope that these pages are providing you with
not only the boost, but also enough support and
encouragement to help you get rolling.

See, when we can shift out of the way that is no
longer serving us, we plug a leak that's been draining
our power in a slow, insidious way. Yes, it will take
extra energy on the front-end, I can't deny that. But

once you've done it, you end up saving yourself years or decades of frustration, sorrow, anger and disappointment.

I know it's hard to summon the energy to make the change. Fear can do that to us—it can block even the most expansive of changes. I also know, however, how much better things will be once you've found the strength to get that proverbial rock rolling down the hill.

Looking In:

It's time to loosen up some stuck-ness around the specific changes you know you want to make in your life.

> 1. Envision one of the changes you want to make, but haven't gotten around to yet. Write it down.

> 2. As you envision this desired (but not yet manifested) change, it's likely that you have a subtle physical reaction to the thought. Gently prod around, with your mind, to feel or see where this reaction has occurred in your body. Where are you suddenly tight or tense? Or perhaps you experience it as a dull ache or mild flutter. Just look/feel around. Write down anything you notice.

3. What shape, size, and color does it have?

4. Does it have a message? What is the message?

If you received any specific insights or messages, take a moment to write those down as well. We'll continue working on this exercise in a minute.

When I'm in a private session with clients, I have the time and space to take this exercise a lot further. Through a guided visualization and other techniques, we shift and alchemize the fear or block. The information gained through this type of body-scan is invaluable, as it offers a mirror to what's really going on inside of us. It does so in a way that circumvents all the stories we typically put up to explain away, or evade, the fear.

For now, know that by simply getting familiar with it in the way you just did—discovering it, learning where it exists within you, and listening for any messages it may have for you—you're taking much of your power back from it.

Digging Deeper

Take another look at what you just wrote in Looking In. Now that you know this fear a little better, the next step is—you guessed it—to send it some love. And not just human-love; invite Divine Love to be part of this process. Send it a beam of light, and literally imagine particles of light seeping into it. Bless the fear, and bless yourself. You've worked hard because of this fear, but now you're choosing to let it go, and to step into something different.

I love the title of the book *Feel the Fear and Do It Anyway*. It is a fabulous and welcome reminder that there will be fear—around change and other things—and that we can choose to keep moving forward even in the face of the fear. Fear doesn't need to be interpreted as a signal for us to stop. Instead, we can learn to see it as a sign that we're on the right track.

For me, I remind myself that I'm experiencing fear because I'm stretching into something new. When I look at it that way, I see fear as a cheerleader, letting me know that I am growing, that I am indeed changing.

Before we end this chapter, let's take a moment to think about this from a spiritual perspective. Every single time you and I step into something new, we are actively participating in the leading edge of creation, because every time we create change in our lives, we are calling new things into existence.

In the big picture, our spiritual journey is about change. That's why we're here—to have new experiences, so that our souls can expand and grow.

When we change, we are fulfilling our purpose for being here. Imagine that!

CHAPTER TWELVE

Beyond Newton

> *There is so much more to your*
> *world than meets the eye. So much*
> *more than your mind can*
> *understand. Your only job is to*
> *allow that this 'more' exists, and to*
> *let it guide your way.*

I've been saying in different ways through the course of this book that to be truly successful at manifesting, we need to add something more than what's being taught in the typical Law of Attraction books. In those, we learn that when we use right-thinking, positive intentions, energetic alignment and visualization of positive outcomes, then we will manifest our desire.

Period.

End of story.

But that's not the end of the story.

Before I go on, I want to reiterate—in order to make it abundantly clear—that I believe 100% that these techniques are critical for manifestation. They are, at the deepest levels of reality, the way we create our lives. I believe this—I know it—so fully that I've devoted the better part of this chapter to offering a ground-breaking understanding of how manifestation happens in the unseen realms of the Universe.

So yes, our thoughts are what manifest our reality.

Leading-edge physicists are saying it; those who have had brushes with death are saying it; every enlightened leader/teacher throughout history has been said it all along. At the core functioning of the Universe, our thoughts become our things.

We see what we believe.

There is, ultimately, no refuting it.

This is all true.

And yet ... given our current state of awareness and belief, it simply is not enough.

Say what?

Listen, we have been taught from the day we were

born to believe in the physical sciences. We were taught that when you want to move an object, you reach out and move it.

Think for a moment: when you were a baby, did you learn from anyone that in order to get a toy, all you had to do was think, "The toy is in my hand?"

I believe I hear a resounding "no" from all corners of the planet.

We have been thoroughly indoctrinated in the belief that physical objects move physical things.

This book offers another illustration of this concept: I had to write it in order for it to "exist." And you had to read it in order for you to "know it." The examples, of course, are endless, and for obvious reasons. We live in a physical world, and we practice (almost) exclusively our physicality.

Our dominant reality is our *physicalness.*

It is classic Newtonian physics, and we were brought up on it as the truth, as *the way things are*.

(Side note: I believe some ancient cultures "knew" other "truths" which is why magic, shapeshifting, miracle-healing etc. happened regularly in their physical reality. But that's another book altogether.)

Let's play devil's advocate for a quick moment. We did all learn about magnetic forces in school. It's likely we found it really cool—perhaps even vaguely magical—that magnets can impact an object without ever touching it. And some of us even learned about quantum physics, which includes the bit about wave-particle duality, which, in a nutshell, illustrates that thoughts have a measurable effect on physical reality.

One could argue, therefore, that we were indeed taught some Law of Attraction principles.

The only problem here is that these were isolated, stand-alone examples—taught in a closed, limited environment (a science classroom). They were never reinforced throughout our day-to-day lives as the way that all parts of the universe exist.

Instead, we were conditioned—day in and day out, moment in and moment out—with the exact opposite; that to affect change, we must literally move things in the physical world.

With any luck, you can now understand my assertion that it's a really, *really* tall order for any of us to be able to flip an entire lifetime of conditioning on its head. And that's what it would take, to fully believe that "all it takes is our thoughts in order to change our physical reality."

Frankly, such a 180-degree shift is pretty much impossible.

This single awareness was a game-changer for me.

It was the light bulb that made me see why the Law of Attraction is so right, and yet seldom works in the way that we want it to.

In our current belief system, thoughts alone are simply not enough to change our physical world. And that is no fault of our own, but rather a simple extension of our life-long conditioning.

We simply are not there yet.

Given this reality, *we need a new way.*

It is time for us to step into the fullness of our actual, current truth. We believe the Law of Attraction works *and* we believe that we must act in the physical world in order to change things in the physical world.

It is not an either/or.

It is a yes/and.

It's both.

So. Let's. Start. Behaving. That. Way.

This is the new way.

And that is why this book exists.

You hold incredible power in this moment, knowing that both sides of the coin are equally real, and that both sides must be acted upon in order for you to be the powerful manifestor that you were born to be.

What does this mean for us? It means that the Law of Attraction still plays a fabulous and wonderful part of our lives! It means our meditative practices, our intention-setting, our guided visualizations all have major roles in manifesting our goals.

It also means that it's time to choose deliberate, consistent actions for the long-term. These actions must be tightly aligned with our goals. And we must keep doing them.

This, my friends, is the crux of this book. You must think your dream into reality *and* you must take consistent, long-term, deliberation action. That is your Practice.

The Deepest, Cosmic Truths about Why Your Practice is the Key

Remember when I talked about my friend Ken Elliot, and how he "sent thought-images" to his telepathic friend Judy Goodman? Judy would then see the forms being created in the space in front of her.

That was the first example I wanted to share in order to help you see that our thoughts are real, viable entities.

This is the next one.

The next story takes Ken's work a giant leap further. It is, in fact, the keystone on which my entire understanding of manifestation is built. It forever changed my relationship to all that the Law of Attraction books were discussing, and provided me a real frame of reference for making sense of it all.

This is a story from my friend William Buhlman, or Bill, as I now know him. Bill's seminal book *Adventures Beyond the Body* appeared to me in the most random of ways. It literally fell on my lap.

Of course that's how it would go, right?

Bill has been practicing Out of Body Exploration for more than 40 years, and he wrote about his experiences in *Adventures*. It is not an exaggeration when I say that as I read *Adventures*, my entire world-view came into vivid focus. All that I'd known and studied of spirituality, quantum physics, science and religion suddenly fit together in a package of awareness and understanding that, frankly, I never really expected to have.

For those of you unfamiliar with Out of Body Exploration (OBE), it is a state in which our conscious awareness separates from our physical body. It has happened across cultures, across religions, and across millennia. You may have heard of similar episodes known as Near Death Experiences (NDE).

In both cases, people find themselves outside of their

bodies, looking back at themselves or the scene, and are entirely conscious and aware. In fact, they invariably describe themselves as being *more* aware, *more* alive, *more* conscious than they are when they're "awake" in their "real life." They often say "real life" feels like a very limited, dream-like state compared to the awareness they experienced while out of body.

There are countless examples of OBEs and NDEs throughout history. They all say the same thing, just in different cultural stories and frameworks.

Bill's approach to OBEs has always been based in curiosity, never attached to religion, and very clearly inquisitive in nature. To me this matters greatly, as it indicates he is objective and has no agenda other than to explore and to share what he's learned. I've also had the pleasure of studying with him directly, which further solidified my belief that he is the real deal. His objectiveness always resonated with the scientist in me, and has helped me to access his insights without fear that he was twisting or exaggerating his experiences.

One of the key stories I've always remembered Bill telling is one in which he watched something being built, in the non-physical world, during his OBEs.

Here's what happened.

Bill and his wife decided to renovate the fireplace in their den. They hired the contractor, worked up the plans, chose the stones, and the project was set to begin in two weeks. As it happened, the fireplace was in the room where Bill practices his OBEs.

One night, as he drifted out of his body during an OBE, he could see, as always, the foggy representation of his den (this first layer of non-physical reality, often called the astral realm, looks almost exactly like the physical world). To Bill's great surprise, he saw the new fireplace, partially built, here in his OBE—in the non-physical world—even though work had not yet begun on the "real" fireplace. During the next couple of weeks, each time he went out of body, that fireplace was built higher and higher, until finally it was complete. Soon thereafter, the contractor came and built it in "real life."

What Bill witnessed during those OBEs is that things are literally built in the non-physical realm first, before they come through into the physical world.

In other words, we are creating a thing long before it comes into our experience.

This paradigm-shifting realization helps me to wrap my head around—on a *deeeeep* level of understanding—the truth behind The Power of Practice.

If we stay with something for just a short while, we do not give it sufficient time and energy to fully form in the non-physical. This means it can't solidify into the physical world, because it's not "done" yet. When we abandon a Practice, we abandon that which we were attempting to manifest. It's as simple as that.

On the flip side, if we stay with something long enough—if it receives enough sustained focus, attention, action and belief, then it has no choice but to appear in the physical world.

This is how creation works.

This is how thoughts become things.

This is how manifestation truly happens.

CHAPTER THIRTEEN

Discipline: It's Not a 4-Letter Word

Take a moment to clear the path.
The clarity and openness will be a
welcome tailwind on your journey.

Elaine came to coaching at the sort of transitional point in her life when many clients find me.

She was forty-one years old, and things were shifting in big ways. She'd had a long career in a field that no longer appealed to her, and she was making progress on the new career of her dreams - but it was slow progress. Her marriage had ended in divorce, and though she wanted to believe in love, getting back into dating only made her feel more alone. Her ex had kept their home, and Elaine felt a bit displaced, caught between a desire to travel and a yearning for a new place to call home.

Elaine worked hard at everything she did, and she
believed in the Law of Attraction, but minor
successes seemed to always be followed by setbacks.

Prior to our first coaching session, I asked Elaine to
imagine that I was a magic genie who could grant her
three wishes. What three things did she really want to
manifest in her life?

Elaine arrived with the following written on a piece
of paper…

Three wishes I would like granted through my
coaching sessions with 'magic genie' Julianna:

> 1. A steady stream of financial
>   prosperity through work I love.
>
> 2. My own home(s), in a place (or
>   places) where I am in a climate I
>   enjoy, surrounded by natural
>   beauty. A sanctuary for me and my
>   pets.
>
> 3. A satisfying, easygoing romantic
>   relationship with a soulmate.

No biggie, right? Just three little things
encompassing, oh, *all one can achieve in life on this
planet.*

I recognized pretty quickly, though, that Elaine was
willing to do the work. She was open to looking at her

life, identifying what was—and what was not—working, and adjusting her approach accordingly. She understood that the Law of Attraction works in concert with action.

At one point, she emailed me a meme of a fitting proverb:

As you pray, move your feet.

Together, using the very exercises in this book, we cleared the path, and Elaine undertook Practices that changed her life in big ways.

How big?

At the time of this writing, less than a year has passed since Elaine began coaching with me.

Less. Than. A. Year.

Here's what's changed for Elaine:

1. She fully retired from the career she'd outgrown and is now earning most of her income in the career of her dreams. She's turned her hobbies into sources of supplemental income.

2. She moved cross-country to live in a beautiful place that had thrilled her in her travels.

3. She fell in love with a man she describes as a soulmate, and is enjoying the most effortless, satisfying romantic relationship of her life.

Um, yeah.

That's how good this stuff is.

When I ask clients the "magic genie" question, my goal is to prompt them to simultaneously dream big and hone in on the most pressing changes they want in their life. I've seen time and again that when I work with clients, the Energy Coaching opens up truly magical results in their lives.

Much of this is the Energy Coaching itself—the very process I've been guiding you through in the pages of this book.

But the other part, as you know very well by now, is their own "I'm *in*" commitment.

I tell you the story of Elaine to inspire you, and also to highlight the importance of the dedication she put into the process. She did not sit idly by, nor did she abandon herself when the going got tough.

Because we all know how exciting it can be to set ourselves on the path of something new. But after the initial feel-good thrill, the practicing part isn't always so enthralling.

And yet *this* is where the rubber meets the road.

It's where you decide how badly you really want a thing.

It's when you ask yourself, as Elaine did, "When is my fire going to outweigh my fear?"

Discipline is Not a 4-Letter Word

I came from an almost comically undisciplined life, to something dramatically different. I mean yes, I was task-oriented and able to get a lot of stuff done. But I was nowhere near uber-disciplined, like those super-go-getters you hear about. I've come a long way though, to know that a committed Practice is crucial for the big wins we want in life.

See, as an Energy Coach and Healer, I am witness to the magic of even the every-day-person becoming more disciplined. Every time I work with a client, we develop activities, guided visualizations, schedules—whatever it takes for them to finally make the changes they want in their lives. My clients are inspired and motivated, yes, but rarely are they the uber-disciplined type. Rather, they are like you and me.

The beautiful thing is that even these little shifts end up working in a big way.

It dawned on me at one point that I am a professional provider-of-and-believer-in discipline. I've seen it work too many times to ever doubt it again.

That said, it can still feel like a four-letter word to me!

Yes, even now.

Here's how intense it was for me at one point: I couldn't ever remember what the word was.

No joke.

I can't tell you the number of times I'd be in conversation, and I would end up stumped, saying, "You know, it takes... oh man... what's that word that starts with a C, or maybe a D, and it's about being consistent? And you show up every day, and you do the thing, again and again and again. What's that word?"

I kid you not. I had a full-on Dead Zone around the word 'discipline.'

Yeah, that's how bad it was.

It's gotten better over time, but trust me, it has taken some work. When I began this book, the writing became my Practice, my discipline. It was my own way to show up, day in and day out. I knew the energy within these pages would propel me forward, and that the mere act of the Practice would make my forward movement exponentially faster.

And it did. For a bit. Until "something came up," and I got distracted. My manuscript sat on the shelf for months. And then for an entire year. So much for my Practice. So much for discipline! But eventually I took my own sage advice and got back on the horse (more on this later). This book is living proof that it is not easy to stick with something all the way through to the end. And yet it was the only way I was ever going to get these insights into the world, as I was being asked to do.

I tell you this story to remind you, yet again, that you are not alone in any challenges you've had with keeping up a Practice in the past. Many of us have been right there with you.

But it can be done.

Dissolving Excuses Before They Arise

We are a stone's throw away from choosing your Practice and getting started.

I know how committed you are, and I know you just want to launch straight into this *I-am-so-excited-and-ready-let's-do-this!* place. I know that feeling well— it's filled with power, and it feels great! And we absolutely want to use that gold to weigh down the left side of that old-fashioned balance scale of yours.

But before you take that last step of choosing your Practice, it's really important to take one last look at the right side of your scale. Very often, hanging out quietly on that side of the scale, is some old energy called "this hasn't worked in the past."

If we leave this energy where it is, it could very well tip your scale in the wrong direction, especially if the thrill of your gold wears off after a few days or weeks. Instead of letting that happen, we're going to take just a few minutes to clear it.

Looking In:

Go ahead and start a fresh page in your journal. Write every response you can think of to the following questions:

1. Why aren't you currently in a Practice toward your goal? Write every single reason, excuse, explanation you have as to why you're not currently in your Practice.

2. What kept you from it yesterday? What's keeping you from it today?

3. If you've tried doing this Practice before, how long did you stick with it?

4. What got you off-track?

5. What will be different this time? (I prompt you with some great ideas for this in the next few chapters.)

6. What will you do to prioritize your Practice in spite of what happened before? (Again, I help with this in the coming chapters.)

7. How long are you willing to allow yourself a "break" to deal with the challenges that may arise? One week? One month?

8. What will you do to make certain you get right back to your Practice?

There! You've made a preliminary strategy to deal with the things that could throw you off your game. As I said, I'll guide you in creating a full and solid game plan, complete with bribes and treats, in the upcoming chapters.

So, let's get to it.

It's time to choose your Practice.

In other words: *Let's get this party started!!*

CHAPTER FOURTEEN

Let's Get This Party Started!

> *When we are open and aligned, we allow the magical workings of Source into our lives.*

My friend, you've come a long way!

I suspect that when you began this book you were ready to jump in, head-first, and just get going on your Practice. I understand—I tend to operate the same way.

Hopefully you've seen the value of reading through and doing the exercises. As you did, you tapped into a level of power and energetic clarity that will *catapult* you toward success. Here's a rundown of what you've already accomplished:

- You shifted and loosened up old patterns

- You created and built up your own personal supply of gold

- You got to know, and release, all the stuck energy that might get in the way of moving forward

- You tapped into an infinite supply of power and guidance

- You learned the deepest, cosmic-level secrets of manifestation

What an awesome journey you've already been on! I promise you that your life will shift simply because of what you've already done. And it will shift exponentially more, once you create (and stick with) your Practice.

I'm so honored to have been your guide through all of it, and I deeply admire your courage and commitment to making this happen. You could have bailed or cut corners (and heck, maybe you did). But what matters is that you're still here. This shows persistence and commitment. It shows tenacity. It shows that you believe in yourself and in your dreams.

You believe enough to put your faith in this process, to do the work, and to dig deep into your truths.

Looking In:

{Fair warning: the exercises in this chapter may take more time than the previous ones, because it's the heart of choosing your practice. You may want to make sure you have an hour or so, uninterrupted, so that you can stay in the flow of its energy.}

In a moment you're going to create your Dream List.

This is a list that will contain all that you're dreaming of in your life right now—the changes you want to make and the new habits you want to form. If you feel like it, keep your Dream List handy and look at it every week or every month. When you do this, you're keeping good vibes around each item on the list.

Obviously, you can't address all of them at one time (at least, I hope that's obvious by now). But you can come back and check off the ones you've completed. And you can keep the dreams of the others alive and active in your consciousness. This helps keep them moving, keeps them in the "creation mode" in the non-physical world.

In fact, I recommend you write a note at the top of your Dream List that says something like, "Dear Universe: Even though I'm committed to focusing on just one of these at a time, please start setting them all in motion so that they arrive in my life easily and serendipitously. It's time for me to have, be, or do these things. Thanks in advance for helping bring them to me."

Once you've created your Dream List, you're going to pare it down to one single Practice. I'm going to walk you through the process right now. And as you'll see, it's going to be pretty easy.

Let's get started!

1. Your Dream List: Write a list of all the changes, things, or goals you would *love* to create in your life. Write and keep writing. Don't edit or second-guess anything—write it all down! Keep going until you're out of desires.

2. Since we want this list to be exclusive to positive, expansive shifts, let's double-check that nothing else got onto the list. Review your list for any "should's" that accidentally made in onto the page. Turn to a new page and copy all of the should's there, under the title of Should List. Once you're done, go back to your original page and cross each of them out.

3. Now, on another new page, rewrite the other items, the ones you didn't cross out. This is your Dream List. We want a clean, fresh energy to this list!

4. Read through your Dream List, and
    notice which ones feel best, easiest,
    most open, most joy-filled. Notice
    too the ones feels like a challenge,
    but are invigorating nonetheless—a
    challenge you are excited to take
    on. Notice the items you're jazzed
    about, that feel good. Put a * in
    front of all of these items. These
    are the items that give you a sense
    of "yes!" and "I'm ready to do
    this!" This energy is very
    important as we set out on this
    journey. It is the energy of success.
    It has the power to get you started,
    and most importantly, it has the
    power to carry you through.

5. Notice the items you resisted.
    Perhaps you tightened a little at the
    thought of them, or perhaps real
    fear came up. Perhaps they feel too
    big for you right now, or maybe
    you've tried them before and
    you're afraid to fail again. There is
    nothing wrong at all with these
    reactions. Rather, those are
    powerful signals that it's not quite
    time to get to work on those
    particular items, and that is
    perfectly okay.

Here's the thing: if we were to attempt those items

right now—the ones that make you feel heavy, draggy, scared, resistant—then it would foil our whole plan (too much weight on the right side of the balance scale!). Instead, we will wait until you have enough success under your belt—enough "success momentum," going for you. Then you will have the power to take on these more challenging tasks.

Remember when I shared the sunglasses metaphor? I said I had another one, and here it is. Envision that these changes—the ones that seem to big to tackle— are giant boulders. If you are to try to push them out of the way, two things will happen: 1) They won't budge, and 2) You'll exhaust yourself.

That's exactly what happens when we try and make a change that is currently too big for us to make—we exhaust ourselves mentally, emotionally, and sometimes even physically.

On the other hand, when we build up our success momentum, it's like getting a shrink-ray gun, or perhaps like becoming a weight lifter; when you come back to those boulders, something magical has happened so that you can suddenly move them— almost with ease!

This is why I'm a big fan of not tackling the "big" stuff head on, or right out of the gates. Instead, I shelve those things for when we're further along the success cycle. At that point, you will likely nail them almost effortlessly. And more importantly, it will be a shift that stays around for the long-term.

I know it sounds crazy, but trust me on this one. That's part of the magic of this approach.

So go ahead and shelve any of those items that caused you to contract. You can come back to them at another point in time. You're not saying "never," you're just saying "not now."

This is a very powerful exercise in using your power and energy wisely. It's a deliberate, strategic move.

Okay, onto our next step.

> 6. Choose your favorite ten (10) items on your Dream List (don't worry about putting them in any order). These are the items that feel like they'll be the easiest and/or most-rewarding.

If you don't have ten, that's completely fine. The more important thing is that you don't have more than ten! Along these lines, you may notice some of your items overlap, and you can easily merge them into one. For instance, if your list says "dance" and "walk" and "yoga" - you can combine them into one Practice called "move my body," to encompass all three options. This gives you the freedom to do whichever one you're most aligned with on a particular day, while upholding your Practice in an easy, downstream way. If you notice such overlaps, go ahead and merge them now.

7. Once you've chosen your Top 10
    (or less) items, write them as a new
    list. Look at each of the items.
    How do they make you feel?
    Excited? Hopeful? Empowered?

8. Now we're going to take this one
    step further, and have you narrow
    the list even further by ranking
    each of them on a scale from 1-10,
    with 10 being "totally, yes!" and
    one being "eh, not so much." For
    each question below, write your
    ranking next to each item.

    a. How *excited* am I to do this
        task every day for the next
        21 days or more?
    b. How *likely* am I to do this
        task every day for the next
        21 days or more?

The goal here is to take an honest look at where your
energy is around each item. In case you haven't
noticed yet, my goal is to set you up for success! All
too often we take on more than we are able to handle,
and this sets us up for failure. That lands us in the
failure cycle and nothing drains motivation faster than
being trapped in the failure cycle.

So you want to hit that sweet spot of being sure that
your Practice feels easy and fun enough that you will
succeed, thereby ushering you into the success cycle.

Your motivation then expands even further, once you're in the success cycle!

Now, for the moment of truth. Go ahead and choose the item that scored the highest. To determine this, take the average of the two numbers you wrote for each item on your Top 10 list.

For instance, if one of the items scored 10 on excitement, and 2 on likelihood, your average score for that item is a 6. If another item scored a 9 on excitement and a 7 on likelihood, you can see it has a much higher average (8) than the first example. You're therefore far more likely to be successful with the second item. And since the success cycle is what we're after, the second item is the place for you to start.

If you find you have a few that tie for first-place, take a few minutes to go inward to find your "best fit."

Here's how you do that.

It's an exercise I love to do with clients (or friends, or myself) when they are trying to choose between different paths forward. I call it the Expansion/Contraction game.

Close your eyes and hold one of your potential Practices in your mind. Note how it makes you feel inside. Do you expand or contract at the thought of doing it regularly for an extended period of time? Now clear that Practice from your mind, and move on to the next. Again, how much do you expand or contract? By doing this with each of your final options, typically one will filter into the foreground as the one that really causes the biggest "expansion." Don't question it or over-think it, but rather believe in your intuitive response.

This is your place to start!

If you really can't find an obvious "winner," then rest assured knowing that any of the options are going to be a great fit for you. Go forth with a clear mind that you had more than one great opportunity, and you're lucky for it. Once you are successful with the Practice of your first item, then you can come back to pick up the next one. There's abundance, right there!

Congratulations!

You have found your Practice!

I hope you take a moment to bask in a sense of accomplishment at having come this far in the process. You've done so much up to this point, and you have truly paved the way for your Practice to be more successful than it ever has been in the past. What an amazing thing!

In the next Chapter we're going to set you up with the precise tools to make sure that the next 21 days (and beyond) are as easy as humanly possible.

Note: It includes treats and other incentives, so *please*

please please keep on reading!

CHAPTER FIFTEEN

A Tail Wind

> *When one needs a reminder of how*
> *to live and create in this world, all*
> *one has to do it watch an animal*
> *or a child, for they flow with the*
> *energy at all times.*

It feels great, doesn't it, knowing you have found your Practice?

I can't tell you how tempted I am to end the book here, in this space of such uplifted vibration, joy, and possibility!

I know major shifts occur in this heightened vibration.

That said, I can't in good conscience walk away from

you quite yet.

Because here's the thing: *it's not enough.*

In the same way that Law of Attraction is not enough (by now you know you simply must add in an equal amount of action), being in this current state of enthusiasm and empowerment is not enough. Not if you want to make your practice truly successful.

I know what it feels like to be on this high, to be inspired—literally to be "in spirit"—and to be filled with a sense of such great possibility. It is the definition of empowered. I think back to one of the first retreats I attended, more than 10 years ago now, and remember how "shifted" I felt when I returned home from it. I had a new belief in my abilities as a healer, and my connection to my higher self had been opened wider than ever before. Determined to carry these qualities with me, I re-entered my "real life" with a new sense of myself.

It lasted for about two days.

I cringe to even write that, but I do it for a very important reason. There was no homework from that retreat, no re-entry or integration tips. There was nothing tying it to, nor merging it with, my everyday life.

And the truth is, this book—and the powerful shifts you have made during the course of this book—will similarly fade away if you don't have the tools and encouragement to carry yourself past the thrill of this initial phase.

Everything you've done thus far has shifted things for you, to be certain. But to get the major, life-changing shifts I believe you're looking for? Those will come when you stay committed to your Practice by prioritizing it.

How do you do that? Well, that's what this chapter all about.

Incentives, Rewards, Bribes & Treats

I want to start with a fun, dynamic approach to helping ensure that you stick with your practice, even after you put this book down. Because even in the midst of discipline, you can still have a whole lot of fun. In fact, it's super-important to make sure your Practice doesn't feel too arduous, which is why we spent so much time in the previous chapter making sure you were powerfully and positively aligned with the Practice you were choosing.

Another way to make it fun is to bribe ourselves.

"You're really telling me to bribe myself?"

Yes.

That's exactly what I'm saying.

"Shouldn't we be strong enough to stay committed to our Practice without such juvenile tricks?"

Bah!

We might be on a spiritual path, but we're still as human as the next person.

Anyway, let me ask you how well that put-your-head-down-and-just-do-it-and-stop-complaining thing has worked for you in the past? I don't say this to be sassy, but rather to check in with how this strategy has served you, or not, over a significant period of time.

I joke, but the truth is, incentives and rewards are powerful tools for motivation. Let's be honest—even as adults we work within an incentive and reward system everywhere we turn. What's your incentive for getting up for work each day? You might get fired if you don't. And your reward for staying at work all day? A paycheck!

Would you do any activity if there wasn't an incentive and/or reward? Even appeasing a "should" is a highly motivating incentive, because it removes the uncomfortable feelings of guilt or shame.

When we look at it this way, we see that we are constantly navigating a series of incentives and rewards. Our task here is to build up a strong enough reward system around your Practice that you're really excited to stick with it.

Looking In:

Pen and paper, please!

Make a list of all the "treats" you would love to have. Don't be shy—write them all down. Some might seem too big, but write them anyway—they can be your long-term-success treats, and boy won't they be a great incentive to help you stay on track!

Make note of which one you want to give yourself at the end of your first day or week. The second week? The first month? The first 3 months?

We all know how good it feels to be positively-rewarded for a job well done. We also know, at this point, how much you've already put into your Practice. So let's go ahead and be good to you.

The rewards don't have to be big, although they could be. Make sure they don't stretch your budget (of time, money, energy, etc.), or else they might backfire unexpectedly if you end up resenting or over-indulging.

I've included a sample list below, to help get you brainstorm some ideas.

Sample Treats and Rewards

- a bubble bath

- a massage

- pint of raspberries

- dinner out with friend/partner

- sleeping in

- a new journal

- new pens

- a set of drum sticks and a drum pad

- sailing lessons (or any other lesson you've been wanting)

- a vacation to a place you've been longing to go

- movie night

- an afternoon alone

- a pedicure

- new shoes

- life coaching (to further your dreams!)

- mango sorbet

- a piece of jewelry to commemorate your Practice

- yoga classes

- a new album (are they even called that anymore?)

- a day at the museum

There's a ton of value in setting yourself up with both short-term and long-term rewards.

Why? Because sometimes it takes a while to see the results (*hello, losing that second 10 pounds*), and an incentive will give you an added boost when your internal motivation is running low.

Remember, your biggest task here is to keep focused and motivated for the long-haul.

It's this precise ability to stick with your Practice, over the long-term, that makes the difference between, "I was totally on a roll... but then something came up," and, "Woo-hoo! I can't believe I *finally* made those changes I've been trying to make for so long!"

One last thing. Please know that these rewards are not cheating, nor are they a sign of weakness. Rather, they are a sign of being smart, savvy, and strategic! Inner rewards work for some things, for some people, at some times. But they don't work for everyone, on everything, all the time.

So we're outsmarting the system during those times that it's about to fritz out on us. We're making a few small adjustments in order to create a way that works, once and for all.

Clearing a Space in Your Schedule

In order to succeed with your Practice, it's imperative to schedule it into your calendar.

Yes, I'm aware of how fundamental and therefore ridiculous this sounds.

But you'd be surprised by how often this tiny-little no-brainer will take a person down.

Seriously, this is one of the biggest things people forget to do when they set out on their Practice. They may schedule it for a week or two, but then it drops off—or gets bumped off—their calendar.

Let me say it again: scheduling your Practice is a must-do!

If you don't, then there's a super-high likelihood that, despite all the effort you've put in so far, you will not be able to sustain your Practice for more than a few weeks.

I don't like to even say that, to put such energy into the world. But I know how true it is, and I simply have to call a spade a spade. Think back to all the places in this book we've talked about the need for stick-to-it-ness. To my mind, it is the actual secret behind the secret. And this scheduling piece is the real-life, on-the-ground way you're going to keep your Practice in the foreground of your life.

Digging Deeper:

Grab your journal and pen. This time, also grab your calendar or scheduler.

(If you don't currently use one, I recommend that your initial Practice is "keeping a schedule." Without it, it's far too easy to stray, get distracted, over-schedule, or un-prioritize your Practice.)

If this seems pedantic to you, I'm going to let you in on a little something. The process that I'm about to walk you through is one of the most crucial parts of coaching—and you're getting it here, for free.

We'll start with your journal.

1. How many times a week will you do your Practice?

2. On a scale from 1-10, how reasonable is this?

3. Which days (and time of day) will you do it?

4. How long will your Practice take on these days?

5. What might get in your way of completing your Practice on these days?

6. What will you do if such a conflict arises?

7. Will that allow you to complete the target number of days that you've committed to?

Work through exercises 5-7 until you've landed on a plan that works.

Once you've settled on a realistic number of days, and the time of day you'll do your Practice, it's time for your scheduler.

1. Add your Practice, for an entire week, on the days/times you've committed to. Be sure to block out any buffer time (travel, for instance, or a shower if it's a physical activity).

2. Check with yourself. On a scale from 1-10, how do-able is this? If it's below a seven, rework it until it's seven or higher.

3. Fill out an entire months-worth of your Practice in your schedule.

4. At the end of that month, place a new item in your schedule titled "Schedule my Practice for next month."

I know, I know, I know!

But if you don't fill those time-slots with your Practice, chances are they will be filled with something else. How many times has that happened to you in the past? I could write an entire chapter on this one specific pitfall.

This scheduling thing is non-negotiable.

Period.

Before we go, one last thing on scheduling:

If you love the Practice you've chosen, but find that you simply don't have the time in your day or week to commit to it, it's time to get really, really honest with yourself. If you want change, and you want it bad enough, then something has got to give.

If you're finding this to be a stuck-spot for you, then grab your journal and pen, and do the following exercise. If not, jump ahead to the next section on Accountability.

1. Go back in your journal and take a look at the list of things (from Chapter 7) that are currently commanding your time and energy. Is each and every one of them more important than your goals?

2. Check off each item that is more

critical (for you to currently
prioritize) than your dream.

3.   Are there any left unchecked? If
     yes, this is where you can loosen
     up some space for yourself. It
     might be a little difficult, but re-
     read your Gold Letter and you'll
     remember why you're doing this,
     why you're changing things up.
     Yes, it's that important.

After doing this, you may discover that you really
don't have the time, space, or extra energy in your life
for a new Practice right now, and that is okay too. I
know it might feel disappointing, especially if you
were excited by your gold. But know that you have
planted many powerful seeds, and they will grow in
time.

Remember all the energetic shifts we've made
throughout this book? They are working their magic,
and as long as you don't abandon hope or effort, the
time for your Practice will indeed arise. Stay
connected to your gold, re-read this book and your
Dream List, and just watch what happens!

And if you did find a couple ways (even if they're
vaguely uncomfortable) to prioritize your goals and
dreams over your busy to-do list right now—
congratulations! That's one of the biggest steps most
people fail to take on their journey.

Accountability

I've long held that about 50% of the power of coaching comes with the accountability of showing up each week to focus on moving forward. Those who hire a coach have a sincere commitment to themselves, and a genuine investment in creating something new in their life.

I believe that you have this same quality. I also believe that you are already really good at being accountable.

That said, I wonder if you're great at being accountable to others, but perhaps not so awesome at being accountable to yourself.

Think for a moment about all the tasks you accomplish, and commitments you fulfill, in the course of a day. Why do you get them done? Are they for you, or for others?

Most of us are pretty good at being accountable when other people are involved. Make a date to help a friend? You're going to show up. Get your kids to soccer practice? Done. Show up for work? Yup. Hand in that report on time? Check.

On the flip side—and I'm pretty sure you know where I'm going with this—when we're doing something that is only for ourselves, we tend to un-prioritize it. Other things comes up, and our self-date (Practice!) gets edged out for "more important" things. Or, we simply forget, having lost interest in the process because it was taking months instead of the hoped-for weeks.

All of this points directly to a gap in accountability. It is highly likely that if your past Practices fell off the rails, it's because you weren't able to stay accountable to this thing you wanted for yourself.

You did not consider "you" and your to be a "good enough" reason to keep your Practice as a priority.

If you are to make your Practice work, we've got to find a way for you to be, and stay, accountable to it.

This is one of those steps in your Practice that I can only advise you on—I can't do it for you. But I've made a list of some great ideas (see below) that you can use. Accountability is key! Choose one or more options that feel good to you.

More Digging Deeper!

1. What will you do to stay accountable this week?

2. What will be your signal that you're faltering in your commitment that you and your Practice are worth it?

3. What will you do if/when you

notice that happening?

For the record, it's perfectly okay to shift accountability strategies mid-stream. The key is to make sure you have something in place, each week, that keeps you in your Practice and deliberately moving toward your focused goal.

- Find an accountability partner. Check in at the beginning of each week, and provide a list of your goals for the coming week, and your accomplishments from the past week. Be sure to choose someone who is of similar intensity to you—it doesn't always work well to pair a hare with a rabbit! It also doesn't work to pair up with someone who might feel like they're nagging (a spouse, a parent), because even if that's not their intention, you might well interpret it that way and unwittingly halt your progress.

- Sign up for a class. If you want to do more art, sign up for an art class so that you double-down on your commitment to practicing. The same holds true for exercise, nutrition, photography, and anything else you might want to do.

- Join a group - but only if they have the same level of commitment to their

Practice as you do... otherwise they might slow you down or hold you back.

- Put an accountability app on your phone. There are some really good ones nowadays, and they can really help you remember your Practice. You get a sense of achievement by checking off or "swiping" each time you've done your Practice.

- Keep tabs on your Practice on social media. Some people find they do really well by being held publicly accountable. I'll be honest and say that this doesn't work for me—I'm far too private for it—but I know others who've had a lot of success with it.

- Beef up your bribes! Have a weekly reward, if that's what it takes.

- Use a journal to track and record your progress. This is especially good for those who are more private about their goals. Just make sure you add "write in journal" to your calendar. Check in at least once a week, just as you would an Accountability Partner.

Remember, your goal here is to stay in positive, can-do energy around your Practice, and to keep at it for weeks, perhaps months, on end. Your Practice is a long-term commitment, and so you want to have as much support as possible to keep your head in it the game.

And the good news is that once you create the habit of your Practice, you won't need as much support staying accountable to it. Instead, it will almost become second-nature.

The next two chapters offer a super-important heads-up about two *crucial* junctures you might find yourself at. They are places that could easily derail you, despite the awesome momentum and enthusiasm you might now have.

Remember: we often enter a Practice with exactly that—big momentum and enthusiasm—and when that peters out (as it naturally does with anything), we fall off our Practice.

Not this time!

These next two chapters are here to help make sure that you get back on the horse (in case you fall off), and you don't drop your Practice just because a new, sexier, shinier option comes along.

Adapt or Die Out

That's the biology dork in me coming out.

It's true for a species, and it's also true for our

Practice. In spite of our best efforts at creating a Practice that totally suits you, there will likely come a point where your current Practice just doesn't seem to work.

This happens because our life circumstances change ("my son now has baseball at 5:00 on weekdays, so I can't work out at that time anymore"), or because we ourselves change ("I thought I'd love meditating, but it really isn't my thing").

The trick here is to adapt, so that our Practice doesn't die out.

Rather than dropping the workouts or the meditation altogether, this is our signal that it's time to shift gears. Maybe you have to shift your workouts to the morning, or perhaps your best bet is to go for a run during the baseball practices. And even if you decide meditation isn't your thing, maybe you realize gardening brings you into that same peaceful space you were hoping to find by meditating, so you shift your Practice to be gardening.

See, as much as it's important to push ourselves a bit to keep up with our Practice, if we find that it really, truly isn't working, then it's time to change it up.

Keep in mind, however, that many of us love to chase Bright and Shiny Objects (BSO) and use that as an excuse to drop our Practice. Be sure that's not what you're up to. (More on Bright and Shiny Objects in the next chapter. If you know that you are a BSO-chaser, be sure to keep reading!)

Instead, these adaptations are for when your Practice
no longer fits into your life. If and when that happens,
then yes, make some changes so that your new
version of your Practice is an easy fit!

CHAPTER SIXTEEN

Falling off the Horse

> *It is our calling as humans to
> create a juxtaposition of light and
> dark, failure and success, love and
> hate so that we can experience the
> gift of the human existence. It is
> also our job as humans to decide
> which of those energies we choose
> to exist in.*

At this point, I can pretty much guarantee you that you're going to keep up this Practice longer than most other self-based goals you have attempted in the past. The energy in this book—and the collective energy of all who are reading it—are lifting you. Like a wave, they are carrying you forward.

This is beautiful, this collective! I am happy beyond

measure to be part of what it's creating for!

And I hope you can feel it, this collective uplifting.

Take a moment to close your eyes, take a deep breath, and breathe in all the "let's do this!" energy of those who have come to this process before you, and those who have yet to arrive. Feel that wave of light and positive momentum lifting you, allow it to fill you and bring you a deep, committed power.

Ahhh... it felt good to drop into that space even while writing those lines!

The Moment(s) of Truth

So ... have you had a chance to do your Practice yet? How many days (or weeks or months)? How's it been going?

Really, how's it been going?

Even if you only chose your practice 20 minutes ago, put an appointment in your calendar to come back to this page in one week. And again in another week. Schedule a check-in with this page for every week of the next 3 months.

(If that seems like a lot of check-ins, for a long time, you can consider it part of your love-filled accountability plan. Also, ask yourself how much you want the change that your Practice will bring. How

big is your fire? Perhaps return to your "Gold" letter
if you find yourself wavering.)

Here's what I want to remind you—whether you
nailed your Practice this week, or if you accidentally
dropped it for a bit: *every single time that you take a
step toward your dreams, you are a success.*

Every time you think an "I can" thought, that is
success. It doesn't matter how big your "I can"
thoughts are, just that you have them, that you are
your own supporter.

The "I can" doesn't come from a place of ego—it's
not forced, nor is it forceful. Rather, it is a deep,
quiet, loving type of knowing. It is filled with
compassion and understanding. It is an "I can" that is
older than you are, older than the earth itself. It is
wise beyond wisdom, and loving beyond any love
you have ever known.

See, success comes in all shapes and sizes. It doesn't
matter what your dream is, only that you are honoring
its presence in your life by determinedly moving
toward it.

Falling off the Horse

I've been drilling it, I know.

Practice.

Practice, practice, practice.

That is the The Way.

I know that you know that by now.

Here's what you might not know: you're going to fall off the horse.

Say what?

Yup.

It is very, very, very likely that you will drop your Practice. For a week. For a month. For six months. We all get interrupted, regardless of our best intentions. Life happens. Things change. There's no way around it.

On a side-note: for the few and rare uber-disciplined among us, this may never arise. Once they commit, they allow nothing to get in their way or throw them off their horse. Nothing. Do you recall my story earlier about Wayne Dyer, and how he ran 10 miles - every single day - for 15 years. That means no sick days. No snow days. No get-out-of-jail-free days. It means, he pulled up his bootstraps every single day without exception. He was uber-disciplined.

Some people can do this.

The rest of us... we just aren't that intense. And that's totally cool, not a problem at all (unless you compare

yourself to the uber-disciplined, because if you're
simply not wired that way, then you're setting
yourself up for disappointment instead of success).

The rest of us? We need a Plan B.

Plan B is for when we fall off the horse, when we
drop our Practice. Without a Plan B, we will most
likely fall of the horse and stay there. We will allow
our Practice to dissolve, because we'll feel like we've
failed.

With a Plan B, however, those derailments become
nothing but temporary little pauses.

Here's how it tends to go, if we only have a Plan A:

"I am soooo excited about this new Practice
[program, technique etc] that I'm doing! I hereby
proclaim (perhaps even by announcing it on social
media) that I'm going to do my Practice every day for
40 days. It will change my life, and I am genuinely
thrilled. Please, if you want to join me, drop me a
note, it's going to be unbelievable!"

All of this is true. And exciting. And you're
genuinely, totally committed.

Then a week passes:

"What an absolutely amazing week! I can't believe
the changes I'm already seeing in my life. I did my
Practice every day this week, and have a new lease on

life. It is beautiful, and magical, and I am so grateful."

Yes! We love this! And it really does happen. You do your Practice every day, and things shift in stunning ways. You've started a positive feedback loop, and the initial momentum of seeing these changes has you thrilled and more committed than ever. Awesome!

"Week 2 was almost as incredible as Week 1. I only missed 2 days, and people at work have started asking me what's different in my life. It feels soooo good. I'm eternally grateful that I have found this Practice. I feel so blessed."

Depending on who you are, and what life circumstances are happening, this scenario plays out for another week, or maybe even a month or two.

And then... well, then it just gets too hard to carry on through all the interruptions in our schedules, the other priorities in our lives. Our commitment wanes, because our Practice loses the luster of "new and exciting."

When this happens, our once-joyous spiral of positive reinforcement disappears. We might even start to believe that the Practice (especially if it's a new technique or program) doesn't really work after all.

Perhaps we stop there. Perhaps we're lucky enough to pick up a new book, a new program, a new technique, and start the cycle again: enthusiasm and joy; commitment and results; interruptions, boredom, and faltering; falling off the horse.

I know this cycle intimately, because it was my own until I realized that the secret is not the technique or program. The secret is the upkeep. It is the maintenance. It is the discipline.

The Practice.

The Way = The Practice

It is the process of getting back on the horse, as quickly as we can, every time we've fallen. And it is the process of returning to that very same Practice, each and every time (until you've reached success and are ready to move onto your next Practice).

Here's Plan B. Remember, Plan A was to not fall off the horse in the first place. If and when Plan A fails, and we fall off our Practice, we go straight to Plan B.

1. Notice that I've fallen off horse

2. Accept—without judgement - that I've fallen off horse

3. Remind myself that not every day is going to be amazing, enlightening, and super-fabulous - but that I committed to stick with it for the long-haul

4. Get back on horse

5.   Thank horse for sticking around and
     waiting for me. Make a plan for how to
     stay on horse longer this time. Why
     did I fall off? What can I do to avoid
     that next time?

Plan B is what keeps us from stalling out or dropping
out. It's what keeps us in the long-term game of
making real change. It elevates our Practice from
pursuing our dreams as a "hobby" to something that
involves the real level of commitment it takes to see
our goals through to the end.

Horses get fallen off all the time. The trick is getting
back on them, every single time it happens.

Onward, I say!

Do It Anyway

One more thing before we leave this chapter.

"Remind myself that not every day is going to be
amazing, enlightening, super-fabulous..."

Whaaaa?? For real??

Yes, for real.

Look, it's really easy when the going is easy. It's
really fun when the going is fun. We are motivated
and inspired when we see results, feel our lives shift,

and begin to manifest wonderful things. All that stuff
is thrilling, which gives us the enthusiasm to keep up
our Practice.

It's when the going gets tough, when it's not
particularly fun at the moment, or we're not seeing
miraculous manifestations, that we tend to fall off that
horse—or simply give up and climb off.

Remember, the secret is Practice. Or, to put it another
way: The secret is Doing it Anyway.

Raining? *Do It Anyway.*

Tired? *Do It Anyway.*

Stressful day at work? *Do It Anyway.*

Cat died? *Take a couple days off, and then get back
on horse. Do It Anyway.*

Moving? *Do It Anyway.*

Divorcing? *Do It Anyway.*

So there you are. The great news is that it gets a
whole lot easier as time goes on. Your stints off-the-
horse get fewer and further between, and your "Do It
Anyway" muscles grow a whole lot stronger.

That's the beauty of mastering the art of your
Practice. You will quickly discover that stick-to-it-
ness is far easier than the frustration of wanting and

wanting but not getting. And in the end, it's the very thing that gets you what you so deeply desire.

CHAPTER SEVENTEEN

Bright and Shiny Objects

*The Universe is infinitely creative
and entirely deliberate.*

I probably shouldn't have saved this one for last, because it's a big one. But I did, so here goes.

We often fall off the horse because our focus shifts to a new bright and shiny object (BSO).

What do I mean by a bright and shiny object? I'm talking about the new process, guru, book, diet, class, etc. that always seems to promise it all. BSO's glimmer and sing the Sirens' sweet call.

BSOs are captivating. They're sexy and tempting, and they seem to "have it all." And while part of their allure can be attributed to an impressive sales strategy, very often the thing being sold (process, technique) really has worked miracles for the teacher and their students.

So we turn to them. To one, and eventually to another. And then to a different one. And the pattern repeats itself, over and over again.

I know—I've done it many times myself.

But I'm hoping by now you've already come to see the danger inherent in BSOs. Just like in the Sirens in *The Odyssey*, our modern-day BSOs steer us off-course. They distract us from our mission, from our Practice. Our job, just like Odysseus, is to find a way to restrain ourselves from succumbing to their enchantment.

That's easy for me to say, but let's take a moment to understand why it's a bit harder to actually do.

The truth is, many of you reading this book are pre-disposed to loving BSOs. Many of you are of an artistic, creative or expansive mindset, which means you're eager to learn and do new things. You likely get great joy from starting something new (but might lose interest when it comes down to completing it). There's a certain spark that occurs in the exploration phase, so when a BSO comes along, it's a chance to explore something new. BSOs therefore hold extra allure for you.

Even if you're not a natural BSO-chaser, it's easy to

fall prey to an offering that others are raving about, particularly when you yourself might be tired. Many of you have put in tremendous effort, for a long time. You've been devoted to this life you're working so hard to manifest. From this fatigued state, any hand reaching out to you, offering you salvation, is going to sound mighty good.

Here's what I want to shout from the rooftops:

Remember when I talked about my friend William Buhlman and his experience where he watched his new fireplace being built in the energy form, during his OBEs, before it actually formed in "real" life?

The key here is that it takes time and consistent, deliberate focus to manifest anything! And chasing BSOs is the exact opposite of giving something time and a consistent, deliberate focus.

Here's an example. Imagine you have been following Abraham's *Law of Attraction* (which is one of the highest-vibrating books available, by the way). You've been attempting to manifest a loving partner in your life. You've been visualizing and affirming, and practicing the sensation that he or she is already there by your side. You've been at it for a while now—weeks anyway, maybe even a few of months.

But that loving partner still hasn't shown up.

You know in your heart of hearts that this process should work—something deep in your soul tells you this. So you've stuck with it. Hoping, trusting, praying, believing.

Alas, you're human. And after trying for so long, with no result, you start having some doubts. You begin to think that the Law of Attraction stuff is failing you, and perhaps it's not everything it's cracked up to be, or you're somehow not doing it right, you're not good enough at it. (This is such a disheartening place to be—I know all too well from experience.)

And then you get an email about a new, amazing technique, with students who have seen remarkable results. Everything about it feels so right, so exciting, so invigorating. You start thinking, "My loving partner hasn't manifested yet with the Practice I've been doing... maybe I need a different approach?"

I want to pause here to acknowledge that this makes total sense. How long can we keep beating the drum of one technique - or even the desire itself - if it simply doesn't seem to be working?

This is true, but let's turn and look at it through the lens of what we just talk about—the fact that objects must have enough power, time, and gravitas in the non-physical, thought-based world, before they are "formed" enough to come through into the physical world.

From this angle, we see that the loving partner is absolutely coming into being. He or she is 100% on their way to you. They're just not quite done lining up with you and your life in the non-physical world yet. And until that process is finished, they can't come to you in the physical realm. So even though they are not yet your partner, it doesn't mean they aren't making their way to you, in the magical way that the Universe causes these things to occur. The thought-based version of "the two of you together" is every bit as real as the physical-based version. It's just the invisible, but equally important, first step.

And remember, some things come through faster than others. When we have a higher belief in their place in our lives, we have less resistance to them coming through (think a new sweater or even a vacation). If our belief is lower (think an 80-foot yacht anchored in front of a seaside mansion in St. Barts), we have a bit more resistance. So the amount of time we devote to one manifestation might be bigger than another.

Here's the thing: *The more time, belief, and commitment you've given to it, the more real it is, and the closer it is to coming into the physical realm.*

I know it's frustrating not to know how far along you are in the process—I still feel that way myself sometimes! And this is precisely when we get most tempted to follow the allure of a BSO.

I also know chasing a BSO is one of the biggest mistakes we make, particularly in the self-growth world. There's always a new and seemingly-better technique popping up on our screen of awareness.

But let me put it bluntly. This book will not work if you keep chasing BSOs.

Bright and shiny objects are the antithesis of everything we're talking about here in *The Power of Practice*. They are the undoing of countless Practices, and countless almost-manifested-dreams.

So perhaps, just perhaps, we're all really signing up for two Practices. The first is the awesome Practice you chose. The second is the commitment not to chase BSOs.

Looking In:

Grab your journal and pen, and write a letter to yourself about bright and shiny objects. Use the following prompts if they suit you, or your own approach if that feels better. Begin with "Dear Self, I know it's exciting to try something new, and not always so fun to see things through to the end. I get it…" And then use the following questions to prompt what types of things to be on the lookout for, and what you'll do when they arise.

> 1. What happens inside of you when you see a Bright and Shiny Object?
>
> 2. What happens inside of you when you say "no" to a Bright and Shiny Object?

3. How long are you typically on one Bright and Shiny Object before you move on to the next?

4. How committed are you to the goals of your current Practice?

5. How do you imagine you'll feel if you abandon these goals?

6. How will you recognize when a Bright and Shiny Object starts drawing you in?

7. What are some big ones that you know you'll be tempted to chase?

8. What do you want to do the next time you encounter a BSO?

I can't emphasize enough the importance of resisting the Sirens' call of bright and shiny objects. I implore you to keep in mind the hazards of chasing these glorious-seeming, but Practice-derailing, BSOs. Instead, plug your ears and cover your eyes so you can't hear their temptation. And keep your focus on the limitless value of sticking with your Practice— long enough for it to fully form in your life

I know this might be a big change from the way you've done things in the past, maybe for your entire life. But I know you can do it—your dreams and goals depend on it!

CHAPTER EIGHTEEN

A Serendipitous Start

Soar now, on the wings of grace.

That, my friend, was a lot!

I commend you, I applaud you, I honor you.

By simply picking up this book, you have told the Universe that you are here to make the best of this lifetime. You have sent signals that you are serious about your goals and dreams, and now Source has begun creating those very things, preparing them to take form in your life.

As you continued through the book, clearing and moving energy, you aligned with the most powerful version of yourself. You've also come to see, and hopefully fully believe, that it is your dedicated, unwavering focus on your Practice that will allow your vision to become real.

In some ways, this process requires real work. In other ways, we've set you up to achieve your goals in the easiest, most downstream way imaginable. Because as we cleared those energies that had been previously been blocking you, we opened up the path for things to flow openly, almost effortlessly.

Let me leave you with one last story. It's one of my favorites, because it illustrates how easily change happens when we take the time to pave the way energetically.

Elisa came to me for Energy Coaching because she, like many of my clients, was looking for a way for change in a number of areas of her life. I listened (which, by the way, is one of the greatest gifts we can ever give each other) and asked gentle questions to help create little cracks in the walls that she had built in her decades of being human.

As our time together progressed, these cracks grew bigger as Elisa came to have a better understanding of where her energy was tight and holding her back, and where it was so fluid that she wasn't sticking with her goals.

Today, Elisa describes our work together in this way, "So many things shifted and changed for me. I became a different person—or should I say—more of ME. I respected myself more & understood what my goals in my life were. The constant rediscovering of who we really are on the inside is so very important to feeling happy & fulfilled, and it spreads right on out to the outside. I am proof of that. Thank you so much Julianna for believing in me and encouraging me to go to the 'uncomfortable' spaces & do the work so that I could become ME."

I love all parts of this note. It is, frankly, the type of note a lot of clients send, because this is invariably the depth of the work we do together. But there's a detail in Elisa's story that always causes me an extra grin. She alluded to in the comment, "and it spreads right on out to the outside—I am proof of that."

She's talking about one of the 'side effects' of our coaching work: she lost 30 pounds in three months.

Here's how she put it.

"Over the course of a few months I also lost 30 pounds without really trying. No joke. I never once talked with Julianna about losing weight, but apparently the issue was there in my subconscious and I needed a way to make this change happen. Julianna gave me the tools to do so."

So yeah.

See why I smile?

Elisa might not have focused on weight-loss, but she did fully commit to a Practice of taking care of herself—of believing herself to be worth the $15 to go to a yoga class twice a week, the 20 minutes to journal, or the 2 hours to walk on the beach and look for beach glass. She practiced a balanced way of speaking her truth, and her needs, to important people in her life.

All of this had both direct and indirect impacts on her life. And all of it fed her soul and allowed her to shed the tightness that I believe holds excess weight, unhappiness, disease, and a scarcity-mindset on so many of us.

That is the beauty of this approach.

And *that* is why this book is different. Like I've said before, it's magic lies in the fact that it's an amalgamation of logic and instinct, practicality and intuitiveness, discipline and love.

It is a balancing of two ways of being, and it is this very balancing that will bring such extraordinary power into your life, just as it did Elisa's.

Elisa did the same type of work as I've laid out for you in this book.

You see, your Practice—as we've set it up throughout this entire book - really will bring exceptional results. I have seen it so many times in my own life and in my coaching work, I know it is true.

I know, too, that choosing a Practice—and putting it

to work in your life—is an ongoing process. Use this book. And then use it again. And again.

I hear from many of my clients that they get something different out of each of the exercises when they do them at different points in their lives, and I hope you'll find this to be true for you as well. I hope you will carry this book with you, literally and metaphorically, as you move in the direction of your dreams.

This is my gift to you now.

So much in my life has come to me through serendipity, this book perhaps most especially. I've come to feel that, while I've filled it to the brim with all the exercises and experience of my years of coaching, it is but the beginning, both for you and for me.

We have things to do in this world, you and I.

Good, warm, important, light-filled things.

And now we have a recipe for doing them successfully.

The Way = Practice.

So, let's do it.

Let's Practice. Let's welcome each new day as the precious opportunity it is. Let's focus, and refocus.

Let's do the work. Let's equally enjoy the journey and the successes. And always—always—let's give thanks for wherever we are at.

Because right now, I have to tell you, I feel such gratitude that you've chosen to come along with me on this adventure.

You've got this.

Go.

Be awesome.

And let me know how you're doing, won't you? Links, contact info and all that jazz are available through my web site below. I would love to hear from you.

With much love,

Julianna
www.jriccienergy.com

Acknowledgments

Getting here was no small feat, and if I had the chance to thank every individual who has helped me on my journey, this book would double in length. Instead, I'm choosing to keep it brief.

First is my genius editor K. C. Wilder. Without her expertise and guidance this book not only would be a mess, it likely would not have seen the light of day. I am deeply grateful for her commitment to this project, as well as to the spunk and beauty with which she blesses this world.

I also want to offer a level of divine gratitude to William Buhlman, whose life-long commitment to Out of Body Exploration paved the way for my understanding of the cosmos. Each of us truly are Source energy (no joke!), ceaselessly learning and growing through our time in this physical world. This knowledge has given me access to an inner power that has been my biggest gift in this lifetime. If I were to follow a guru, William would be the one. That said, he would never tolerate followers, so that plan is already out the window.

As for my education as an Energy Healer and Coach, I can't say enough about my coaching alma mater, the Institute for Professional Excellence in Coaching (iPEC). iPEC is a world-leader in coach certification, not only because of their rigorous training, but because it is built on the foundation that a person's own truth and power are the driving force of all greatness. As for my training as a healer, my Reiki Master, Myra Partyka, taught me how to be intimately aligned with Source energy, and has been my trusted friend and mentor. She is a living example of showing up in service, and walking the path of grace.

To Sara Abernethy, thank you for the blessings you wrote for the beginning of these chapters—they amplified (as we knew they would) the presence of Spirit in these pages. Thank you also for the love and compassion that you bring into everything you do and to everyone you touch. My life has changed because of your friendship, and I look forward to these next steps as we both bring our work into the world in bigger and brighter ways.

I want to thank my dearest friends (you know who you are) and my family (you also know who you are) for your endless support during this process, as well as the years and decades leading up to it. I've long held my mission to be "uplifting the collective vibration," and your support has provided that exact uplifting for me.

And finally, my heart goes to the three main men in my life: the brilliant, inspiring Lights that are my two sons, Jasper and Xander; and my eternally patient and enlightened husband. As much as this path has required faith and determination on my part, I believe it's required even more from you. I don't have the words to express my gratitude and love, but please know they are felt, on many, many levels.

About the Author

Acclaimed for her work with clients ranging from musicians and writers, to CEOs and social impact entrepreneurs, Julianna Ricci's Energy Alchemy Coaching is changing the lives of those who are bettering the world.

Julianna began her professional career in a much different fashion: earning her Masters degree as a marine scientist. Clearly her soul had other plans.

Today Julianna instructs coaches, intuitives and holistic practitioners in her signature Energy Alchemy system. The Power of Practice is her means of broadening this reach, so that countless readers have access to these same powerful tools and insights, and can, in their own ways, raise the collective vibration as they bring their Source-given gifts into the world.

www.jriccienergy.com

Made in the USA
San Bernardino, CA
04 October 2018